D0041664

Designing Your Life

Designing Your Life

How to Build a Well-Lived, Joyful Life

Bill Burnett and Dave Evans

ALFRED A. KNOPF   NEW YORK   2016

This Is a Borzoi Book Published by Alfred A. Knopf

Copyright © 2016 by William Burnett and David J. Evans

All rights reserved. Published in the United States by Alfred A. Knopf, a division of Penguin Random House LLC, New York, and distributed in Canada by Random House of Canada, a division of Penguin Random House Canada Limited, Toronto.

www.aaknopf.com

Knopf, Borzoi Books, and the colophon are registered trademarks of Penguin Random House LLC.

Library of Congress Cataloging-in-Publication Data
Names: Burnett, William (Consulting professor of design), author. | Evans, David J., author.
Title: Designing your life : how to build a well-lived, joyful life /
William Burnett and David J. Evans.
Description: New York : Alfred A. Knopf, 2016.
Identifiers: LCCN 2016008862 | ISBN 9781101875322 (hardcover) |
ISBN 9781101875339 (ebook) | ISBN 9780451494085 (open market)
Subjects: LCSH: Vocational guidance. | Self-realization. |
Design—Social aspects. | Decision making.
Classification: LCC HF5381 .B7785 2016 | DDC 650.1—dc23
LC record available at https://lccn.loc.gov/2016008862

Jacket design by Oliver Munday

Manufactured in the United States of America
Published September 20, 2016
Reprinted Two Times
Fourth Printing, October 2016

To all of the wonderful students who have
shared their stories and lives with us and
whose openness and willing engagement
have taught us more about life design than
we ever could have imagined.

To my wife, Cynthia, who told me to take
the job at Stanford; I love you and wouldn't
be the person I am without you.

–Bill Burnett

To my dear wife, Claudia, the true literary
force in our house, who refused to let
me not write this book and has tirelessly
reminded me why. Your love has redeemed
me again and again.

–Dave Evans

Contents

Introduction: Life by Design

Ellen liked rocks. She liked collecting them, sorting them, and categorizing them according to size and shape, or type and color. After two years at a prestigious university, the time came for Ellen to declare her major. She had no idea what she wanted to do with her life or who she wanted to be when she grew up, but it was time to choose. Geology seemed like the best decision at the time. After all, she really, really liked rocks.

Ellen's mother and father were proud of their daughter, *the geology major, a future geologist.* When Ellen graduated, she moved back home with her parents. She began babysitting and dog walking to make a little money. Her parents were confused. This is what she had done in high school. They had just paid for an expensive college education. When was their daughter going to turn magically into a geologist? When was she going to begin her career? This is what she had studied for. This is what she was *supposed* to do.

The thing is—Ellen had realized she didn't want to be a geologist. She wasn't all that interested in spending her time studying the earth's processes, or materials, or history. She wasn't interested in fieldwork, or in working for a natural-resource company or an environmental agency. She didn't like mapping or generating reports. She had chosen geology by default, because she had liked rocks, and now Ellen, diploma in hand, frustrated parents in her ear, had absolutely no idea how to get a job and what she should do with the rest of her life.

If it was true, as everyone had told her, that her college years were the best four years of her life, Ellen had nowhere to go but down. She did not realize that she was hardly alone in not wanting to work in the field in which she had majored. In fact, in the United States, only 27 percent of college grads end up in a career related to their majors. The idea that what you major in is what you will do for the rest of your life, and that college represents the best years of your life (before a life of hard work and boredom), are two of what we call dysfunctional beliefs—the myths that prevent so many people from designing the life they want.

Dysfunctional Belief: *Your degree determines your career.*
Reframe: *Three-quarters of all college grads don't end up working in a career related to their majors.*

By her mid-thirties, Janine was really starting to reap the benefits of decades of dedication. She'd jumped on the fast track early and had managed to stay there. She was a graduate of a top college and a top law school, had joined a firm that did important and influential work, and was on her way to really "making it." College, law school, marriage, career—everything in her life had turned out exactly as she had planned, and her willpower and hard work had given her everything she wanted. She was the picture of success and achievement.

But Janine had a secret.

Some nights, after driving home from the law firm that bore one of the most recognizable names in Silicon Valley, she would sit out on the deck as the lights of the valley came on, and cry. She had everything she thought she should have, everything that she thought she wanted, but she was profoundly unhappy. She knew she should be ecstatic with the life she had created, but she wasn't. Not even close.

Janine imagined that there was something wrong with her. Who wakes up every morning the picture of success, and goes to bed every night with a knot in her stomach, feeling as if there's something missing, something that got lost along the way? Where do you turn when you have everything and nothing all at the same time? Like Ellen, Janine held a dysfunctional belief. She believed that if she rode all the merry-go-rounds and grabbed for all the brass rings she would find happiness. Janine is also not alone. In America, two-thirds of workers are unhappy with their jobs. And 15 percent actually hate their work.

Dysfunctional Belief: *If you are successful, you will be happy.*
Reframe: *True happiness comes from designing a life that works for you.*

Donald had made his money. He had worked for more than thirty years at the same job. His home was almost paid off. His children had all graduated from college. His retirement funds had been carefully invested. He had a solid career and a solid life. Get up, go to work, pay the bills, go home, go to bed. Wake up the next day and do it all again. Lather. Rinse. Repeat.

For years Donald had been asking the same question over and over. He carried this question with him to coffee shops, to the dinner table, to church, and even into his local bar, where a few fingers of Scotch would quiet the question. But always it would return. For close to a decade, the question had woken him up at 2:00 a.m. and stood with him in front of the bathroom mirror— "Why the hell am I doing this?"

Not once had the guy looking back at him in the mirror ever had a good answer. Donald's dysfunctional belief was related to Janine's, but he'd held on to it for much longer—a life of responsible and successful work should make him happy. It should be enough? But Donald had another dysfunctional belief: that he couldn't stop doing what he'd always done. If only the guy in the mirror could have told him that he was not alone, and he did not have to do what he had always done. In the United States alone, more than thirty-one million people between ages forty-four and seventy want what is often called an "encore" career—work that combines personal meaning, continued income, and social impact. Some of those thirty-one million have found their encore careers, and many others have no idea where to begin, and fear it's too late in life to make a big change.

Dysfunctional Belief: *It's too late.*
Reframe: *It's never too late to design a life you love.*

Three people. Three big problems.

Designers Love Problems

Look around you. Look at your office or home, the chair you are sitting on, the tablet or smartphone you may be holding. Everything that surrounds us was designed by someone. And every design started with a problem. The problem of not being able to listen to a lot of music without carrying around a suitcase of CDs is the reason why you can listen to three thousand songs on a one-inch square object clipped to your shirt. It's only because of a problem that your phone fits perfectly in the palm of your hand, or that your laptop gets five hours of battery life, or that your alarm clock plays the sound of chirping birds. Now, the annoying sound of an alarm clock may not seem like a big problem in the grand scheme of things, but it was problem enough for those who didn't want to start each day with the harsh beeping of a typical alarm clock. Problems are why you have running water and insulation in your home. Plumbing was created because of a problem. Toothbrushes were invented because of a problem. Chairs were created because someone, somewhere, wanted to solve a big problem: sitting on rocks causes sore bottoms.

There's a difference between design problems and engineering problems. We both have engineering degrees, and engineering is a good approach to solving a problem when you can get a great deal of data and you're sure there is one best solution. Bill worked on the problem of engineering the hinges on Apple's first laptops, and the solution he and his team came up with made those laptops some of the most reliable on the market. The solution required many prototypes and lots and lots of testing, similar to the design process, but the goal of creating hinges that would last five years (or opening and closing ten thousand times) was fixed, and his team tested many different mechanical solutions until they met their goal. Once this goal was met, the solution could be reproduced millions of times. It was a good engineering problem.

Compare this with the problem of designing the first laptop that had a "built-in mouse." Because Apple's computers relied on the mouse to do almost everything, building a laptop that required you to be wired up to a regular mouse was unacceptable. This was a design problem. There was no precedent to design toward, there was no fixed or predetermined outcome; there were plenty of ideas floating around the lab, and a number of different designs were tested, but nothing was working. Then along came an engineer named Jon Krakower. Jon had been tinkering around with miniaturized trackballs, and had the crazy idea to push the keyboard to the back of the unit, leaving just enough room to squeeze in this tiny pointing device. This turned out to be the big breakthrough everyone had been looking for, and has been part of the signature look of Apple laptops ever since.[1]

Aesthetics, or the way things look, is another obvious example of a problem with no one right solution that designers work on. For instance, there are a lot of high-performance sports cars in the world, and they all evoke a sense of speed, but a Porsche doesn't look anything like a Ferrari. Both are expertly engineered, both contain almost identical parts, but each has a completely different aesthetic appeal. The designers at each company take exquisite care with every curve and line, every headlight and grille, but they make very different decisions. Each company works in its own way—a Ferrari has an unmistakably passionate Italian look, and a Porsche a fast, exacting German sensibility. Designers study aesthetics for years in order to make these industrial products the equivalent of moving sculpture. That's why, in some ways, aesthetics is the ultimate design problem. Aesthetics involves human emotion—and we've discovered that when emotions are involved, design thinking has proved to be the best problem-solving tool.

When we were faced with the problem of helping our students leave college and enter the world as productive and happy people—to figure out just what the hell to do with the life in front of them—we knew design thinking would be the best way to solve this particular problem. Designing your life doesn't involve a clear goal, like creating hinges that last five years, or building a giant bridge that will safely connect to landmasses; those are engineering problems, in which you can get hard data on your options and engineer the one best solution.

When you have a desired outcome (a truly portable laptop computer, a sexy-looking sports car, or a well-designed life) but no clear solution in sight, that's when you brainstorm, try crazy stuff, improvise, and keep "building your way forward" until you come up with something that works. You know it when you see it, whether it's the harmonious lines of a Ferrari or the ultra-portable MacBook Air. A great design comes together in a way that can't be solved with equations and spreadsheets and data analysis. It has a look and feel all of its own—a beautiful aesthetic that speaks to you.

Your well-designed life will have a look and a feel all of its own as well, and design thinking will help you solve your own life design problems. Everything that makes our daily living easier, more productive, more enjoyable, and more pleasurable was created because of a problem, and because some designer or team of designers somewhere out there in the world sought to solve that problem. The spaces we live in, work in, and play in were all designed to make our life, work, and play better. No matter where we look in our external world, we can see what happens when designers tackle problems.

We can see the benefits of design thinking.

And you're going to see the benefits of design thinking in your own life. Design doesn't just work for creating cool stuff like computers and Ferraris; it works in creating a cool life. You can use design thinking to create a life that is meaningful, joyful, and fulfilling. It doesn't matter who you are or were, what you do or did for a living, how young or how old you are—you can use the same thinking that created the most amazing technology, products, and spaces to design your career and your life. *A well-designed life is a life that is generative—it is constantly creative, productive, changing, evolving, and there is always the possibility of surprise.* You get out of it more than you put in. There is a lot more than "lather, rinse, repeat" in a well-designed life.

How Do We Know?

It all started with a lunch.

Actually, it all started when we were both undergrads at Stanford University in the 1970s (Dave a little earlier in the decade than Bill). Bill discovered the product-design major and an exciting career trajectory to go with it. As a child, he used to draw cars and airplanes while sitting under his grandmother's sewing machine, and when he majored in product design, it was because he had discovered (much to his surprise) that there were people in the world who did this kind of thing every day, and they were called designers. As the executive director of the Design Program at Stanford, Bill is still drawing and building things (he's come out from under the sewing machine), directing the undergraduate and graduate programs in design, and teaching at the d.school (The Hasso Plattner Institute of Design—a multidisciplinary hub of innovation at Stanford where all the classes are based on the design thinking process). Bill has also worked in start-ups and Fortune 100 companies, including seven years at Apple, designing award-winning laptops (and those hinges) and a number of years in the toy industry, designing Star Wars action figures.

Bill knows how lucky he was to have discovered product design and a joyful and fulfilling career path so early. In our teaching careers, we've both come to see how rare that is, and just how often it doesn't work that way for students, even at Stanford.

Unlike Bill, when Dave was an undergrad, he had no idea what he was going to do. He failed at being a biology major (more on that later) and graduated in mechanical engineering—frankly, for lack of a better idea. During college, he never found good help with the question "How do I figure out what I want to do with my life?" He managed to figure it out eventually, "the hard way," and has enjoyed more than thirty years in executive leadership and management consulting in high technology. He product-managed the first mouse and early laser-printing projects at Apple, was a co-founder of Electronic Arts, and has helped lots of young start-up founders find their way. After a pretty rough start, his career developed wonderfully—but he always knew that it had been a lot harder than it needed to be.

Even though we both went off to start careers and families, we continued to keep a hand in working with students. Bill was at Stanford, where he watched as hundreds of students came through his office hours and struggled with figuring out life after graduation. Dave was teaching at UC Berkeley, where he had developed a course called How to Find Your Vocation (aka: Is Your Calling Calling?), which he taught fourteen times over eight years. Still, he longed to do more at Stanford. Along the way, he and Bill had intersected time and again, in business and personally. Dave had heard that Bill had just accepted the position of executive director of the Stanford Program in Design, a program Dave knew well. It occurred to Dave that the multidisciplinary demands of being a designer were likely to put design students under an unusually heavy burden: trying to find a way to conceive a personally meaningful and authentic, as well as commercially viable, career vision. He decided to call up Bill and have lunch and share some of his ideas—just to see what might happen. If it went well, maybe they'd have more lunches on the topic, and in perhaps a year or so something might come of it.

And that's why it all began at lunch.

Five minutes into that lunch, it was a done deal. We decided we were going to partner to bring a new course to Stanford, to apply design thinking to designing life after college—first to design students and, if that went well, then to all students.

That course has gone on to become one of the most popular elective classes at Stanford.

When asked what we do at Stanford, we will sometimes respond with our carefully crafted elevator reply: "We teach courses at Stanford that help any student to apply the innovation principles of design thinking to the wicked problem of designing your life at and after university." And, of course, they then say, "Great! What's that mean?"

And we usually say, "We teach how to use design to figure out what you want to be when you grow up." At that point almost everyone says, "*Oh!* Can I take the class?!" For years we've had to say no to that question, at least to everyone who didn't happen to be one of the sixteen thousand students at Stanford. That is finally no longer the case. We've been offering Designing Your Life workshops to everyone (www.designingyour.life), and we've written this book so that you don't have to go to Stanford to have a well-designed life.

But you do have to be willing to ask yourself some questions. Some hard questions.

Designers Also Love Questions

Just as Donald faced the mirror every night and asked himself, "Why the hell am I doing this?," everyone struggles with similar questions about life, about work, and about his or her meaning and purpose in the world.

- **How do I find a job that I like or maybe even love?**
- **How do I build a career that will make me a good living?**
- **How do I balance my career with my family?**
- **How can I make a difference in the world?**
- **How can I be thin, sexy, and fabulously rich?**

We can help you answer all these questions—except the last one.

We have all been asked, "What do you want to be when you

grow up?" This is the fundamental question of life—whether we are fifteen or fifty. Designers love questions, but what they really love is reframing questions.

Reframing is one of the most important mind-sets of a designer. Many great innovations get started in a reframe. In design thinking we always say, "Don't start with the problem, start with the people, start with empathy." Once we have empathy for the people who will be using our products, we define our point of view, brainstorm, and start prototyping to discover what we don't yet know about the problem. This typically results in a reframe, sometimes also called a pivot. A reframe is when we take new information about the problem, restate our point of view, and start thinking and prototyping again. You start out thinking you are designing a product (a new coffee blend and new kind of coffee machine) and reframe when you realize you are actually redesigning the coffee experience (Starbucks). Or, in an attempt to make an impact on poverty, you stop lending money to the wealthy class in a country (as the World Bank does) and start lending money to people considered too poor to pay it back (micro-lending and the Grameen Bank). Or the team at Apple comes up with the iPad, a complete reframe of what the portable computing experience is about.

In life design, we reframe a lot. The biggest reframe is that your life can't be perfectly planned, that there isn't just one solution to your life, and that that's a good thing. There are many designs for your life, all filled with hope for the kind of creative and unfolding reality that makes life worth living into. Your life is not a thing, it's an experience; the fun comes from designing and enjoying the experience.

The reframe for the question "What do you want to be when

you grow up?" is this: "Who or what do you want to grow into?" Life is all about growth and change. It's not static. It's not about some destination. It's not about answering the question once and for all and then it's all done. Nobody really knows what he or she wants to be. Even those who checked a box for doctor, lawyer, or engineer. These are just vague directions on a life path. There are so many questions that persist at every step of the way. What people need is a process—a design process—for figuring out what they want, whom they want to grow into, and how to create a life they love.

Welcome to Life Design

Life design is the way forward. It's what will help Ellen move from her college major to her first job. It's what will help Janine move from the life she should have into the life she wants. It's what will help Donald find the answer to the questions that keep him up at night. Designers imagine things that don't yet exist, and then they build them, and then the world changes. You can do this in your own life. You can imagine a career and a life that don't exist; you can build that future you, and as a result your life will change. If your life is pretty perfect as is, life design can still help you make it an even better version of the life you currently love living.

When you think like a designer, when you are willing to ask the questions, when you realize that life is always about designing something that has never existed before, then your life can sparkle in a way that you could never have imagined. That is, if you like sparkles. It's your design, after all.

What Do We Know?

In Stanford's Design Program, we have taught more than a thousand students design thinking and how to design their lives. And we'll let you in on a secret—no one has ever failed our class. In fact, it's impossible to flunk. We have more than sixty years of combined teaching experience, and we have taught this approach to high school students, college students, graduate students, Ph.D. students, twenty-somethings, mid-career executives, and retirees wanting an "encore" career.

As teachers, we have always guaranteed our students "office hours for life." This means that if you take a class from us we are there for you, forever. Period. We've had students come back to us over the years since they've graduated, and they've told us how the tools, ideas, and mind-sets that we teach have made a difference for them. We're quite hopeful—and, frankly, pretty confident—that these ideas can make a difference for you, too.

But don't take our word for it. Stanford is a very rigorous place. Though anecdotes are nice, they don't count for much in academia. To speak authoritatively, you need data. Our class is one of the few design thinking classes that have been scientifically studied and have proved to make a difference for students on a number of important measures. Two doctoral students did their dissertations on the course, and what they found was pretty exciting.[2] They found that those who took our class were better able to conceive of and pursue a career they really wanted; they had fewer dysfunctional beliefs (those pesky ideas that hold you back and that just aren't true) and an increased ability to generate new ideas for their life design (increasing their ideation capability). All of these measures were "statistically significant," which, in non-geek-speak, means that the ideas and exercises we lay out in our course and are going to walk you through in this book have been proven effective; they can help you to figure out what you want and show you how to get it.

But let's be perfectly clear right from the start. Science or no science, this is all highly personal stuff. We can give you some tools, some ideas, some exercises, but we can't figure it all out for you. We can't give you your insights, change your perspective, and provide you with nonstop "aha" moments, all in ten easy steps. What we can tell you is that if you actually use the tools and do the life design exercises, you will generate the insights you need to have. Because here's the big truth: there are many versions of you, and they are all "right." And life design will help you live into whatever version of you is now playing at the Cineplex. Remember, there are no wrong answers, and we're not grading you. We will suggest you do some exercises in this book, but there are no answers in the back to tell you how you did. We've added a recap of the exercises at the end of each chapter that has them—a Try Stuff box—because we suggest that you, well, try stuff. That's what designers do. We're not measuring you against anyone, and you shouldn't measure yourself against anyone, either. We're here to co-create with you. Think of us as part of your own personal design team.

In fact, we suggest you go out and get a design team right off the bat—a group of people who will read the book with you and do the exercises alongside you, a collaborative team in which you support one another in your pursuit of a well-designed life. We'll talk about this more later in the book, and by all means you should feel free to read it on your own first. Many people think that designers are lone geniuses, working in solitude and waiting for a flash of inspiration to show them the solution to their design problem. Nothing could be further from the truth. There may be some problems, such as the design of a stool or a new set of children's blocks, that are simple enough to be tackled by an individual, but in today's highly technical world, almost every problem requires a design team. Design thinking takes this idea even further and suggests that the best results come from radical collaboration. Radical collaboration works on the principle that people with very different backgrounds will bring their idiosyncratic technical and human experiences to the team. This increases the chance that the team will have empathy for those who will use what they are designing, and that the collision of different backgrounds will generate truly unique solutions.

This is proved over and over again in d.school classes at Stanford, where graduate students create teams of business, law, engineering, education, and medical students that come up with breakthrough innovations all the time. The glue that holds these teams together is design thinking, the human-centered approach to design that takes advantage of their different backgrounds to spur collaboration and creativity. Typically, none of the students have any design background when they enroll in our classes, and all of the teams struggle at first to be productive. They have to learn the mind-sets of a designer—especially radical collaboration and being mindful of process. But once that happens, they discover that their abilities as a team far exceed what any individual can do, and their creative confidence explodes. Hundreds of successful student projects and innovative companies, such as D-Rev and Embrace,[3] have come from this process, and are proof that collaboration is the way design gets done today.

So be a genius at your life design; just don't think you have to be one of those lone geniuses.

Think Like a Designer

Before you can do life design, you need to learn to think like a designer. We'll explain a few simple ways to do this, but first you need to understand one really big point: Designers don't *think* their way forward. Designers *build* their way forward. What does that mean? It means you are not just going to be dreaming up a lot of fun fantasies that have no relationship to the real world—or the real you. You are going to build things (we call them prototypes), try stuff, and have a lot of fun in the process.

Want a career change? This book will help you make that change, but not by sitting around trying to decide what that change is going to be. We're going to help you think like a designer and build your future, prototype by prototype. We're going to help you approach your own life design challenges with the same kind of curiosity and the same kind of creativity that resulted in the invention of the printing press, the lightbulb, and the Internet.

Our focus is mainly on jobs and careers, because, let's face it, we spend most of the hours of our days, and the days of our lives, at work. Work can be a daily source of enormous joy and meaning, or it can be an endless grind and waste of hours spent trying to white-knuckle our way through the misery of it all until the weekend comes. A well-designed life is not a life of drudgery. You weren't put on this earth to work eight hours a day at a job you hate until the time comes to die.

That may sound a bit melodramatic, but many people tell us that this is a good description of their lives. And even those who are lucky enough to find a career they love often find that they are frustrated and have a hard time designing a life that is balanced. It's time to start thinking differently—about everything.

Design thinking involves certain simple mind-sets. This book will teach you those mind-sets and how to use them to do life design.

The five mind-sets you are going to learn in order to design your life are *curiosity, bias to action, reframing, awareness,* and *radical collaboration.* These are your design tools, and with them you can build anything, including a life you love.

Be Curious. *Curiosity* makes everything new. It invites exploration. It makes everything play. Most of all, curiosity is going to help you "get good at being lucky." It's the reason some people see opportunities everywhere.

Try Stuff. When you have a *bias to action,* you are committed to building your way forward. There is no sitting on the bench just thinking about what you are going to do. There is only getting in the game. Designers try things. They test things out. They create prototype after prototype, failing often, until they find what works and what solves the problem. Sometimes they find the problem is entirely different from what they first thought it was. Designers embrace change. They are not attached to a particular outcome, because they are always focused on what will happen next—not what the final result will be.

Reframe Problems. *Reframing* is how designers get unstuck. Reframing also makes sure that we are working on the right problem. Life design involves key reframes that allow you to step back, examine your biases, and open up new solution spaces. Throughout the book, we will be reframing dysfunctional beliefs that prevent people from finding the careers and the lives they want. Reframing is essential to finding the right problems and the right solutions.

Know It's a Process. We know that life gets messy. For every step forward, it can sometimes seem you are moving two steps back. Mistakes will be made, prototypes thrown away. An important part of the process is letting go— of your first idea and of a good-but-not-great solution. And sometimes amazing designs can emerge from the mess. The Slinky was invented this way. Teflon was created this way. Super Glue. Play-Doh. None of these things would exist if a designer somewhere hadn't screwed up. When you learn to think like a designer you learn to be *aware of the process.* Life design is a journey; let go of the end goal and focus on the process and see what happens next.

Ask for Help. The last mind-set of design thinking is perhaps the most important, especially when it comes to designing your life: *radical collaboration.* What this means is simple—you are not alone. The best designers know that great design requires radical collaboration. It takes a team. A painter can create an artistic masterpiece alone on a windswept coast, but a designer cannot create the iPhone alone, windswept beach or not. And your life is more like a great design than a work of art, so you cannot create it alone, either. You do not have to come up with a brilliant life design by yourself. Design is a collaborative process, and many of the best ideas are going to come from other people. You just need to ask. And know the right questions to ask. In this book, you will learn how to use mentors and a supportive community to help with your life design. When you reach out to the world, the world reaches right back. And this changes everything. In other words, life design, like all design, is a team sport.

Anti-Passion Is Our Passion

Many people operate under the dysfunctional belief that they just need to find out what they are passionate about. Once they know their passion, everything else will somehow magically fall into place. We hate this idea for one very good reason: most people don't know their passion.

Our colleague William Damon, director of the Stanford Center on Adolescence, found that only one in five young people between twelve and twenty-six have a clear vision of where they want to go, what they want to accomplish in life, and why.[4] Our experience suggests, similarly, that 80 percent of people of all ages don't really know what they are passionate about.

So conversations with career counselors often go like this:

Career Counselor: "What are you passionate about?"
Job Seeker: "I don't know."
Career Counselor: "Well, come back when you figure it out."

Some career counselors will give people tests to assess people's interests or strengths, or to survey their skills, but anyone who has taken such tests knows that the conclusions are often far from conclusive. Besides, finding out that you could be a pilot, an engineer, or an elevator repairman isn't very helpful or actionable. So we're not very passionate about finding your passion. We believe that people actually need to take time to develop a passion. And the research shows that, for most people, passion comes *after* they try something, discover they like it, and develop mastery—not before. To put it more succinctly: passion is the result of a good life design, not the cause.

Most people do not have that *one thing* they are passionate about—that singular motivator that drives all of their life decisions and infuses every waking moment with a sense of purpose and meaning. If you've found that studying the mating habits and evolution of mollusks from the Cambrian period until the present day is your purpose for living—we salute you. Charles Darwin spent thirty-nine years studying earthworms; we salute Charles Darwin. What we don't salute is a method of approaching life design that leaves out 80 percent of the population. In truth, most people are passionate about many different things, and the only way to know what they want to do is to prototype some potential lives, try them out, and see what really resonates with them. We are serious about this: you don't need to know your passion in order to design a life you love. Once you know how to prototype your way forward, you are on the path to discovering the things you truly love, passion or not.

A Well-Designed Life

A well-designed life is a life that makes sense. It's a life in which who you are, what you believe, and what you do all line up together. When you have a well-designed life and someone asks you, "How's it going?," you have an answer. You can tell that person that your life is going well, and you can tell how and why. A well-designed life is a marvelous portfolio of experiences, of adventures, of failures that taught you important lessons, of hardships that made you stronger and helped you know yourself better, and of achievements and satisfactions. It's worth emphasizing that failures and hardships are a part of every life, even the well-designed ones.

We're going to help you figure out what a well-designed life looks like for you. Our students and clients tell us it's fun. They also tell us that it's full of surprises. We can assure you that at times it will take you out of your comfort zone. We're going to ask you to do things that may feel counterintuitive, or at the very least different from what you've been taught in the past.

Curiosity
Bias to action
Reframing
Awareness
Radical collaboration

What happens when you do these things? What happens when you engage in life design? Actually, something quite extraordinary happens. Things you want start to show up in your life. You start to hear of job openings you were dreaming about. People you were interested in meeting just happen to be in town. What is happening here? For starters, it's that "getting good at being lucky" thing we mentioned earlier, a result of curiosity and awareness, and a by-product of using the five mind-sets. In addition, the process of discovering who you are and what you want has a rather extraordinary effect on your life. There will be effort and action involved, no doubt, but it will seem, rather surprisingly, as if everyone is conspiring to help you. And, by being aware of the process, you will have a lot of fun along the way.

All through the process of life design, we will be right here with you. To guide you. To challenge you. We're going to give you the ideas and tools you need for designing your way through life. We're going to help you find your next job. Your next career. Your next big thing. We're going to help you design your life. A life that you love.

Designing
Your Life

1

Start Where You Are

here's a sign over the design studio at Stanford that says *You Are Here.* Our students love that sign. You might say it's somewhat clarifying. It doesn't matter where you come from, where you think you are going, what job or career you have had or think you should have. You are not too late, and you're not too early. Design thinking can help you build your way forward from wherever you are, regardless of the life design problem you are facing. But before you can figure out which direction to head in, you need to know where you are and what design problems you are trying to solve. As we've shown, designers love problems, and when you think like a designer, you approach problems with an entirely different mind-set. Designers get juiced by what they call wicked problems. They're called wicked not because they are evil or fundamentally bad, but because they are resistant to resolution. Let's face it, you're not reading this book because you have all the answers, are in your dream job, and have a life imbued with more meaning and purpose than you can imagine. Somewhere, in some area of your life, you are stuck.

You have a wicked problem.

And that's a wonderful and exciting place to start.

Problem Finding + *Problem Solving* = *Well-Designed Life*

In design thinking, we put as much emphasis on problem finding as we do on problem solving. After all, what's the point of working on the wrong problem? We emphasize this because it's actually not always so easy to understand what our problems are. Sometimes we think we need a new job or a new boss, but often we don't really know what's working and what's not in our lives. Often we approach our problems as if they are an addition or subtraction problem. We either want to get something (add) or get rid of something (subtract). We want to get a better job, get more money, get more success, get more balance, get rid of ten pounds, get rid of our unhappiness, get rid of our pain. Or we might just have a vague sense of discontent, or a feeling that we want something different or something more.

Usually, we define our problem by what's missing, but not always. And the bottom line is this:

You've got problems.

Your friends have problems.

We've all got problems.

Sometimes those problems relate to our job, sometimes to family, or health, or love, or money, or any combination of these things. Sometimes our problems can feel so overwhelming that we don't even try to solve them. We just live with them—like an irritating roommate we constantly complain about but never get around to evicting. Our problems become our story, and we can all get stuck in our stories. Deciding which problems to work on may be one of the most important decisions you make, because people can lose years (or a lifetime) working on the wrong problem.

Dave had a problem once (okay, he's had a lot of problems, and would say that this whole book comes out of his astonishing ineptitude), but this particular problem kept him stuck for years.

Dave started college at Stanford as a biology major, but he soon realized not only that he hated biology but also that he was failing miserably. He had graduated from high school believing that it was his destiny to be a field-research marine biologist. There were two people responsible for this particular version of Dave's destiny—Jacques Cousteau and Mrs. Strauss.

Jacques Cousteau was his childhood hero. Dave watched every episode of *The Undersea World of Jacques Cousteau* and secretly imagined he had been the one to invent the Aqua-Lung instead of Jacques. Dave also really liked seals. He ended up believing that the coolest thing in the world would be to get paid to play with seals. Dave was also curious about whether seals had sex in the water or on the land (only with the birth of Google many years later did he learn that most species mate on land).

His second misguided reason for becoming a marine biologist had to do with Mrs. Strauss, his high school biology teacher. Dave did pretty well in all his high school subjects, but he liked biology the best. Why? Because he liked Mrs. Strauss the best. She made biology interesting; she was a great teacher. And Dave misperceived that her good teaching correlated to his stronger interest. If his PE teacher had taught as well as Mrs. Strauss, Dave might have believed that it was his destiny to hang a whistle around his neck and be an advocate for mandatory dodgeball in the workplace.

So the unholy union of Jacques Cousteau and Mrs. Strauss caused Dave to work on the wrong problem for over two years. The problem he thought he was solving was how to become a marine biologist, or, more specifically, how to inherit the *Calypso* from Cousteau when he died. Dave started college with the firm belief that his future was in marine biology; since Stanford didn't offer a major in marine biology, he decided to major in biology. He hated it. At that time, biology classes consisted mostly of bio-chemistry and molecular biology. The premeds were killing it in class. Dave was not. Academically, he was getting crushed, as were his dreams of someday getting paid to frolic with the seals while speaking in a French accent.

He then decided that, in order to fix his problem of hating biology and doing horribly in his classes, all he needed to do was some real science: research in a bio lab would get him a step closer to researching the mating habits of seals. He crashed his way into doing bench research on RNA, which meant he basically cleaned test tubes. It was crushingly boring, and he was even more miserable.

Quarter after quarter, his bio teaching assistants and lab teaching assistants kept asking him why he was a biology major. Dave would begin to tell them about Mrs. Strauss and Jacques Cousteau and the seals, but they would interrupt and say, "You're no good at bio. You don't like it. You are grumpy and nasty all the time. You should quit. You should drop this major. The only thing you are good at is arguing; maybe you should be a lawyer."

Despite the tsunami of negative feedback, Dave persisted, because he had this set idea in his mind of his destiny, and he kept working away at the "problem" of getting his grades up in biology. He was so focused on the what-he-had-in-mind problem that he never looked at the real problem—he shouldn't be majoring in biology, and his idea of his destiny had been misguided from the beginning.

It has been our experience, in office hour after office hour, that people waste a lot of time working on the wrong problem. If they are lucky, they will fail miserably quickly and get forced by circumstance into working on better problems. If they are unlucky and smart, they'll succeed—we call it the success disaster—and wake up ten years later wondering how the hell they got to wherever they are, and why they are so unhappy.

Dave's failure as a marine biologist was so profound that he ultimately had to admit defeat and change his major. It took him two and a half years to address a problem that was clear to everyone else after about two weeks. He eventually transferred to mechanical engineering, where he was quite successful and happy.

Someday, however, he still hopes to frolic with seals.

A Beginner's Mind

If Dave had known to think like a designer fresh out of high school, he would have approached the problem of his college major with a beginner's mind. Instead of assuming he knew all the answers before he asked the questions, he would have been curious. He would have wanted to know exactly what a marine biologist does, and he would actually have asked some marine biologists. He would have gone to the Hopkins Marine Station of Stanford (only about an hour and a half's drive from campus), and asked how you go from a major in biochemistry to working in marine biology. He would have tried stuff. For instance, he could have spent some time on the open sea and discovered whether it was as glamorous as it looked on television. He could have volunteered on a research vessel, maybe even spent some time around some real-life seals. Instead, he began college with his mind (and his major) made up, and ended up learning the hard way that maybe his first idea wasn't his best.

Isn't that true for all of us? How often do we fall in love with our first idea and then refuse to let it go? No matter how badly it turns out. More important, do we really think it is a good idea to let our earnest but misguided seventeen-year-old self determine where we work for the rest of our lives? And what about now? How often do we go with our first idea and think we know answers to questions we've never really investigated? How often do we check in with ourselves to see if we are really working on the right problem?

"I need a better job" is not the solution to the problem of "I'm not that happy working, and I'd rather be home with my kids." Beware of working on a really good problem that's not actually the right problem, not actually *your* problem. You don't solve a marriage problem at the office, or a work problem with a new diet. It seems obvious, but, like Dave, we can lose a lot of time working on the wrong problem.

We also tend to get mired in what we call *gravity problems.*

"I've got this big problem and I don't know what to do about it."

"Oh, wow, Jane, what's the problem?"

"It's gravity."

"Gravity?"

"Yeah—it's making me crazy! I'm feeling heavier and heavier. I can't get my bike up hills easily. It *never* leaves me. I don't know what to do about it. Can you help me?"

This example may sound silly, but we hear versions of this sort of "gravity problem" all the time.

"Poets just don't make enough money in our culture. They're not respected enough. What do I *do* about it?"

"The company I work for has been family-owned for five generations. There is *no way* that, as an outsider, I'm ever going to be an executive. What do I *do* about it?"

"I've been out of work for five years. It's going to be much harder for me to get a job and that's not fair. What do I *do* about it?"

"I want to go back to school and become a doctor, but it will take me at least ten years, and I don't want to invest that much time at this stage of my life. What do I *do* about it?"

These are all gravity problems—meaning they are not real problems. Why? Because in life design, if it's not actionable, it's not a problem. Let's repeat that. If it's not actionable, it's not a problem. It's a situation, a circumstance, a fact of life. It may be a drag (so to speak), but, like gravity, it's not a problem that can be solved.

Here's a little tidbit that is going to save you a lot of time— months, years, decades even. It has to do with reality. People fight reality. They fight it tooth and nail, with everything they've got. And anytime you are arguing or fighting with reality, reality will win. You can't outsmart it. You can't trick it. You can't bend it to your will.

Not now. Not ever.

A Public Service Announcement About Gravity and Public Service

You've heard the expression "You can't fight City Hall." That's an old idiom about gravity problems. Everybody knows you can't fight City Hall. "Hey!" you retort. "You can *so* fight City Hall! Martin Luther King fought City Hall. My friend Phil fought City Hall. We need *more* City Hall fighters—not fewer! Are you telling us to give up on the hard problems?"

You raise an important question, so it's important to make clear exactly how to address what we're calling gravity problems. Remember that the key thing we're after here is to free you from getting stuck on something that's *not actionable*. When you get stuck in a gravity problem, you're stuck permanently, because there's nothing you can *do*, and designers are first and foremost doers.

We recognize that there are two variations of gravity problems— totally inactionable ones (such as gravity itself) and functionally unactionable ones (such as the average income of a full-time poet). Some of you are trying to decide if the thing you're stuck on is a gravity problem that isn't actionable, or just a really, really hard problem that will require effort and sacrifice and runs a high risk of failure but is worth trying. Let's address this difficult issue by looking at each of the sample gravity problems we listed above.

Gravity Biking. You can't change gravity. You'd have to relocate the earth's orbit to pull that off, and that's a pretty crazy goal.

Skip it. Just accept it. When you accept it, you are free to work around that situation and find something that *is* actionable. That cyclist could invest in a lighter bicycle. She could try losing some weight. She could learn the latest techniques for climbing more effectively (turns out pedaling faster in really small gears is easier and takes more stamina instead of more power; stamina is easier to build up).

Poet Income. To change the median income of poets, you'd somehow have to alter the market for poetry and get people to buy more poetry or pay more for it. Well, you could try for that. You could write letters to the editor in praise of poetry. You could knock on doors to get people out to the poetry night at your local coffeehouse. This one is a long shot. Even though you can work on this "problem" in a way that wasn't possible with gravity, we'd recommend that you accept it as an inactionable situation. If you do that, then your attention is freed to start designing other solutions to other problems.

Five-Year Unemployed Job Seeker. The statistics are unmistakable on this one. If you've been unemployed a long time, you have a harder task to get re-employed. Research using identical résumés with no difference but the duration of unemployment made clear that most employers avoid the long-term unemployed—apparently, groundlessly concluding that whoever else didn't hire you over that time must have had a good reason. That's a gravity problem. You can't change employers' perceptions. Instead of changing how they think, how about working on changing how you appear to them? You can take volunteer roles and list significant professional results (without having to get into how little you were paid until much later in the conversation). You can identify roles in industries where there is less ageism. (Dave is so grateful that he got into teaching later in life; now his age is seen as a source of wisdom, and he's not still trying to pass himself off as a marketing expert to clients half his age who know he's no digital native and doesn't actually "get it" anymore.) Even in the face of daunting realities, you always have some freedom you can exercise. Find it and take action there, instead of against gravity.

The Family Firm Outsider. So, for the last 132 years, no one whose last name wasn't Fiddleslurp has held an executive role in the company, but you think the time has finally come, and you're going be the one to break through. If you just do a great job and bide your time, in three to five years that VP title will be yours. Okay—you can invest those three to five years, but, please, do so realizing that there is no evidence whatever that your goal will be attained. It's your call, but you might be better off buying a lottery ticket. You have other options. You can go down the road, to a firm that's not family-run. But you love the town, and the kids are happy in school where you are. Okay—then embrace the good things that come from just accepting it. Reframe the company's family legacy as being your source of job security, with a decent income, in a dependable firm. Knowing you won't have to take on increased responsibilities in adjusting to endless promotions, you'll be able to learn the job so well you can do it in thirty-five hours a week, resulting in great work-life balance (and time to write more poetry!). Or maybe you look for greater value instead of greater authority. You find a new function or offering that can grow the company or increase profits, and become the expert—the go-to person—for running that part of the business. You will always be a manager and never a VP, but, as the person responsible for so much value, you could become the highest-paid manager in the place. Who needs a title if you're getting paid what you want?

Ten Years to the M.D. Again, this is a real gravity problem—unless you'd like to start your life design project by reforming medical school education (which, by the way, is pretty tough to do if you don't already have an M.D.). No—we wouldn't sign up for that one, either. What you can do is change your thinking and remember that in only your second year of med school you get to start treating patients and "doing medicine." Most of the doctoring done in hospitals is done by the residents—the trainees who have finished four years of medical school and gotten their M.D.s and are now walking the wards and apprenticing. If you can't change your life (because of gravity), you can just change your thinking. Or you can decide to take a different route—be a physician's assistant and do a lot of what doctors do but at a fraction of the training time and cost. Or enter the wellness field, running prevention programs for a progressive insurance company and thereby making a dent on health without being on the clinical-care side of things.

The key is not to get stuck on something that you have effectively no chance of succeeding at. We are all for aggressive and world-changing goals. Please do fight City Hall. Oppose injustice. Work for women's rights. Pursue food justice. End homelessness. Combat global warming. But do it smart. If you become open-minded enough to accept reality, you'll be freed to reframe an actionable problem and design a way to participate in the world on things that matter to you and might even work. That's all we're after here—we want to give you the best shot possible at living the life you want, enjoying the living of it, and maybe even making a difference while you're at it. We are going to help you create the best-designed life available to you in reality—not in some fictional world with less gravity and rich poets.

The only response to a gravity problem is acceptance. And this is where all good designers begin. This is the "You Are Here" or "Accept" phase of design thinking. Acceptance. That's why you start where you are. Not where you wish you were. Not where you hope you are. Not where you think you should be. But right where you are.

The Life Design Assessment

In order to start where we are, we need to break life down into some discrete areas—health, work, play, and love. As we've said, we'll be focusing mostly on work, but you won't be able to understand how to design your work until you understand how it fits into the rest of your life. So, in order to start where we are, we have to know where we are. We do this by taking stock of our situation—by taking our own inventory and making an assessment. It's a way to get an articulated characterization of where we are and answer the age-old question "How's it going?" But first let's define the areas that will ground your answer.

Health. From the earliest days of civilization, thoughtful people have recognized that it pays to be healthy. And by "healthy" we mean being well in mind, body, and spirit—emotional health, physical health, and mental health. The relative importance of each of these aspects of health is up to you. How you measure your own health in these areas is your call. But once you've figured out how you define "health," you need to pay attention to it. How healthy you are will factor significantly into how you assess the quality of your life when answering that "How's it going?" question.

Work. By "work" we mean your participation in the great ongoing human adventure on the planet. You may or may not be getting paid for it, but this is the stuff you "do." Assuming you're not financially independent, you usually are getting paid for at least a portion of your "work." Don't for a minute reduce work only to that which you get paid for. Most people have more than one form of work at a time.

Play. Play is all about joy. If you observe children at play (we're talking more about finger painting with mud than about championship soccer here), you will see the type of play we are talking about. Play is any activity that brings you joy when you do it. It can certainly include organized activity or competition or productive endeavors, but when those things are done "for the joy of it" they are play. When an activity is done to win, to advance, to achieve—even if it's "fun" to do so—it's not play. It may be a wonderful thing, but it's still not play. The question here is what brings you joy purely in the doing.

Love. We all know what love is. And we all know when we have it and when we don't. Love does make the world go around, and when it's lacking, our world can feel like it's not moving us much. We won't attempt to define love (you know what you think on that, anyway), and we have no formulas for finding your one true love (there are *lots* of other books about that), but we do know that you have to pay attention to it. Love comes to us in a wide range of types, from affection to community to eroticism, and from a huge array of sources, from parents to friends to colleagues to lovers, but they all share that people thing. That sense of connection. Who are the people in your life, and how is love flowing to and from you and others?

So — How's It Going?

There is no appraisal or judgment *we* (or anyone) can make of your life in these four areas. We've all needed a remodel in at least one of these areas of life. The idea is to pick what to design first, and be curious about how you might design this particular area of your life. Awareness and curiosity are the design mind-sets you need to begin building your way forward.

The exercise below is going to help you figure out where you are and what design problem you'd like to tackle. You can't know where you're going until you know where you are.

Really. You can't.

Do the exercise.

That's why the sign says *You Are Here.*

The Health/Work/Play/Love Dashboard

A way to take stock of your current situation, the "You Are Here" for you, is to focus on what we call the health/work/play/love dashboard. Think of this like the gauges on your car's dashboard.

Gauges tell you something about the state of your car: Do you have enough gas to complete your journey? Is there oil in the engine to help it run smoothly? Is it running hot and about to blow? Similarly, the HWPL dashboard will tell you something about the four things that provide energy and focus for your journey and keep your life running smoothly.

Dysfunctional Belief: *I should already know where I'm going.*
Reframe: *You can't know where you are going until you know where you are.*

We are going to ask you to assess your state of health and the ways you work, play, and love. Health is at the base of our diagram because, well, when you're not healthy, nothing else in your life works very well. Work, play, and love are built on top of health and represent three areas we think it's important to pay attention to. We want to stress that there is no perfect balance of these areas. We all have different mixes of health, work, play, and love in our lives at different times. A young single person, fresh from college, might

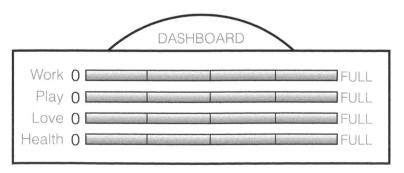

have an abundance of physical health, lots of play and work, but no meaningful love relationship yet. A young couple with children are going to play a lot, but in a different way from when they were single or when they didn't have children. And as we age, health becomes a bigger concern. There will be an appropriate mix for you, and you will have a sense of it, at whatever stage of life you are in.

When you think about health, we suggest you think about more than just a good checkup at the doctor's. A well-designed life is supported by a healthy body, an engaged mind, and often, though not always, some form of spiritual practice. By "spiritual" we don't necessarily mean religious. We call spiritual any practice that is based on a belief in something bigger than ourselves. Again, there is no objective perfect balance of these different areas of health, just a subjective personal sense that either "I have enough" or "Something is missing."

Even though perfect balance is not our goal, a look at this diagram can sometimes warn us that something is not right. Like an emergency light on your car's dashboard, the diagram may serve as an indicator that it's time to pull over and figure out what's wrong.

As an example, an entrepreneur who we know named Fred took a look at his dashboard and noticed that he had almost no entries in the health and play categories. His dashboard looked like this:

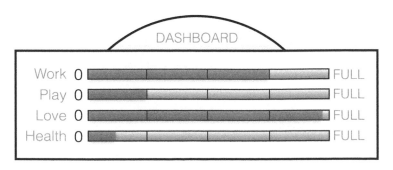

FRED'S DASHBOARD

Fred had been careful to make time for his wife and family—start-ups can be tough on relationships—so he felt good about his love gauge. He was willing to give up most of his playtime, because he was "all in" on his start-up, so the lack of balance there was okay with him. However, the assessment helped him realize that he had gone too far, especially when it came to his health, which was a red light on his dashboard. "To be a successful, high-performance entrepreneur, particularly under the extreme stress of a start-up, I can't afford to get sick. I need to manage my health, even more now that I'm in a start-up." Fred made some changes: he hired a personal trainer, started working out three times a week, and committed to listening to one audio book a week on a challenging intellectual or spiritual subject during his commute. He reported more efficiency at work and a much higher job and life satisfaction with this new mix.

Debbie, a product manager at Apple who recently stopped working to raise her twin boys, was surprised to find her dashboard reassuring. "I thought that, since I wasn't 'working' anymore, I had lost my 'work' identity. I realized that if I properly valued the work I was doing for the household and my kids, then I was actually working more now than before. And I'm taking good enough care of my body and my mind to make sure that I get to

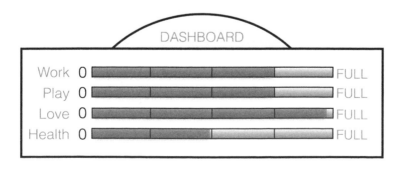

DEBBIE'S DASHBOARD

enjoy my quality time with the twins. This dashboard validates my choice to stop working for money while my kids are little."

So there are Fred's and Debbie's stories; let's get started with your dashboard.

Your Health Gauge

As we said, healthy to us means being well in more than just your body; you might want to take into account your mind and spirit, too. The relative importance of each area is entirely up to you. Make a quick assessment of your health and then fill in your gauge—are you a quarter full, or half, or three-quarters, or really full? (Bill has also filled in the gauges for his dashboard as an example to reference.)

How you rate your health will factor significantly into how you assess the quality of your life and what you might want to redesign going forward.

Health

0 [   ] FULL

Bill's example:

Health: I'm in good general health, had a good physical recently. I have slightly elevated cholesterol, I should lose fifteen pounds to be at my ideal weight, I am not exercising, I am out of shape, and I'm frequently winded if I have to run for the train. I read and write about my philosophy of life, work, and love; I read the latest research on the mind and the mind-body connection, but I am losing my memory faster than I think I should. I say an affirmation every morning, and this has completely changed my outlook on life. I have been in an intentional men's group ever since my son was born (twenty-one years ago), and these men have been my guides and companions on many spiritual journeys. I rate my health as "half full."

0 FULL

Your Work Gauge

Make a list of all the ways you "work," and then "gauge" your working life as a whole. We are assuming that there are things on your list that you are getting paid to do. This will include your nine-to-five job, and your second job if the first isn't enough, and any consulting or advising you do, etc. If you are a regular volunteer in any organization, figure that in, too. If you are a homemaker, like Debbie, make sure you remember that raising children, providing home-cooked meals for your family, taking care of aging parents, and doing housework are all forms of "work."

Work

_____

_____

0 ▭▭▭▭▭▭▭▭▭▭ FULL

Bill's example:

Work: I work at Stanford and do some private consulting, I teach Designing Your Life workshops, I'm on the board of VOZ, a socially responsible start-up (noncompensated).

0 ▰▰▰▰▰▰▰▰▱ FULL

Your Play Gauge

Play is about activity that brings joy just for the pure sake of the doing of it. It can include organized activity or productive endeavors, but only if they are done for fun and not merit. We contend that all lives need some play, and that making sure there is some play in our day is a critical life design step. Make a quick list of how you play and then fill in your gauge—are you a quarter full, or half, or three-quarters, or really full?

Play

0 ▭▭▭▭▭▭▭ FULL

Bill's example:

Play: I play by cooking meals for friends and throwing big out-door parties—but that's kind of it.

(By the way, Bill considers this to be a *red light* on his dashboard.)

0 ▬▭▭▭▭ FULL

Your Love Gauge

We do think that love makes the world go around, and when we don't have any, our world isn't as bright and alive as it could be. We also know that we have to pay attention to love, and that it arrives in a wide range of forms. Our primary relationship is where we go first for love, children typically come next, and then it's a flood of people and pets and community and anything else that is an object of affection. And it is as critical to feel loved by others as it is to love—it has to go both ways. Where is the love flowing in your life, from you and from others? Make a list, and then fill in your gauge.

Love

_____

_____

0 ▢▢▢▢▢▢▢▢▢FULL

Bill's example:

Love: Love shows up in a lot of places in my life. I love my wife, my children, my parents, my brothers, and my sister, and I receive love back from all of them in their own ways. I love great art, painting especially, and it moves me like nothing else. I love music in all its forms—it can make me happy and can make me cry. I love the great spaces in the world, man-made or in nature, that take my breath away.

A look at Bill's dashboard highlights the lack of play and some issues with physical health. These "red lights" are indicators of areas that Bill may need to attend to.

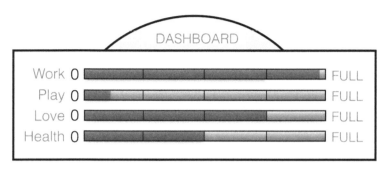

BILL'S DASHBOARD
with "RED LIGHT" on PLAY and HEALTH

So—How's It Really Going?

Knowing the current status of your health/work/play/love dashboard gives you a framework and some data about yourself, all in one place. Only you know what's good enough or not good enough—right now.

After a few more chapters and a few more tools and ideas, you may want to come back to this assessment and check the dashboard one more time, to see if anything has changed. Since life design is an iterative process of prototypes and experimentation, there are lots of on ramps and off ramps along the way. If you're beginning to think like a designer, you will recognize that life is never done. Work is never done. Play is never done. Love and health are never done. We are only done designing our lives when we die. Until then, we're involved in a constant iteration of the next big thing: life as we know it. So the questions remain: Are you happy right now with where your gauges stand in each of these four areas? Have you looked at them honestly? Are there areas that need action? Have you perhaps come up against one of your wicked problems? That is possible, even this early in the process. If you think you have, make sure to check first for a "gravity problem." Ask yourself if your problem is actionable. Also, look for some expression of balance and proportionality in your dashboard—very important for design—without imagining that there is some perfect symmetry or balance between all the areas in your life. It's unlikely that health, work, play, and love will divide neatly into four equal parts. But when life is really out of balance, there can be a problem.

Bill noticed that his play gauge was way too low. How's yours? Is your play gauge at a quarter and your work at full or more? What about love? What about your health? How is your mental health, and your spirit? We're guessing you are already starting to get a feel for the areas in your life in need of some design or innovation.

As you begin to think like a designer, remember one important thing: it's impossible to predict the future. And the corollary to that thought is: once you design something, it changes the future that is possible.

Wrap your mind around that.

Designing something changes the future that is possible.

So, although it is not possible to know your future, or figure out a great life design before you begin, at least you have a good idea of your starting point. Now it's time to get you pointed in the right direction for the journey ahead. For that, you'll need a compass.

Try Stuff
Health/Work/Play/Love Dashboard

1. Write a few sentences about how it's going in each of the four areas.

2. Mark where you are (0 to Full) on each gauge.

3. Ask yourself if there's a design problem you'd like to tackle in any of these areas.

4. Now ask yourself if your "problem" is a gravity problem.

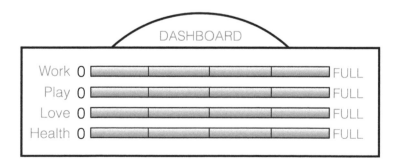

2

Building a Compass

We have just three questions for you:

What is your name?

What is your quest?

What is the airspeed velocity of an unladen swallow?

If you're like most people, it was probably easy to answer two of those three questions. We all know our names, and a simple Google search can give us the other answer—twenty-four miles per hour. (For all of you hard-core Monty Python fans, that velocity is for a *European* swallow.)

So let's talk about the question that's a little bit harder—what is your quest? It's not hard to imagine that if we added up all the hours spent trying to *figure out* life, for some of us they would outweigh the hours spent actually *living* life. Really. Living. Life.

We all know how to worry about our lives. Analyze our lives. Even speculate about our lives. Worry, analysis, and speculation are not our best discovery tools, and most of us have, at one time or another, gotten incredibly lost and confused using them. They tend to keep us spinning in circles and spending weeks, months, or years sitting on that couch (or at a desk, or in a relationship) trying to figure out what to do next. It's as if life were this great big DIY project, but only a select few actually got the instruction manual.

This is not designing your life.

This is obsessing about your life.

We're here to change that.

And the questions we're ultimately asking are the same ones the Greeks started asking in the fifth century b.c. and we've all been asking ever since: What is the good life? How do you define it? How do you live it? Throughout the ages, people have been asking the same questions:

Why am I here?

What am I doing?

Why does it matter?

What is my purpose?

What's the point of it all?

Life design is a way for you to figure out your own answers to these perennial questions, and to figure out your own good life. Dave's answers to "Why am I here?" and "What am I doing?" and "Why does it matter?" are going to be different from Bill's answers, and our answers are going to be different from yours. But we are all asking the same questions. And we can all find answers for our own lives.

In the last chapter, you answered one of our favorite questions— "How's it going?"—a question we often ask in our office hours. If you filled in your life design dashboard, you now know where your gauges are full, and where they're running on empty, and knowing what's on your life design dashboard is the first step in designing your life.

The next step is building your compass.

Building Your Compass

You need two things to build your compass—a Workview and a Lifeview. To start out, we need to discover what work means to you. What is work for? Why do you do it? What makes good work good? If you discover and are able to articulate your philosophy of work (what it's for and why you do it), you will be less likely to let others design your life for you. Developing your own Workview is one component of the compass you are building; a Lifeview is second.

Now, Lifeview may sound a bit lofty, but it's really not—everyone has a Lifeview. You may not have articulated it before, but if you are alive, you have a Lifeview. A Lifeview is simply your ideas about the world and how it works. What gives life meaning? What makes your life worthwhile or valuable? How does your life relate to others in your family, your community, and the world? What do money, fame, and personal accomplishment have to do with a satisfying life? How important are experience, growth, and fulfillment in your life?

Once you've written your Workview and your Lifeview, and completed the simple exercise that follows, you'll have your compass and be on the path toward a well-designed life. Don't worry—we know that your Workview and Lifeview will change. It's obvious that the Workview and Lifeview you have as a teenager, as a young college grad, and as an empty nester will all be substantially different. The point is, you don't have to have it all figured out for the rest of your life; you just have to create the compass for what life is about for you right now.

Parker Palmer, a renowned educational reformer and author of

Let Your Life Speak, says that at one point he suddenly realized he was doing a noble job of living someone else's life. Parker was emulating his great heroes—Martin Luther King, Jr., Gandhi—both great social justice leaders of the 1950s and '60s. Because he valued their sentiments and goals, he set his path in the world by their compass, not his own, and worked hard to change the educational system from within. He earned a Ph.D. at UC Berkeley and was on track to reach his goal of becoming a respected university president. That was all well and good, but Parker hated it. He came to the realization that he could be inspired by people like Martin Luther King and Gandhi, but that didn't mean he had to walk their same path. He ended up redesigning his life as a thought leader and writer—still working for the same goals, but in a way that was less about imitation and more about authenticity.

The point is, there are lots of powerful voices in the world, and lots of powerful voices in our heads, all telling us what to do or who to be. And because there are many models for how life is supposed to be lived, we all run the risk, like Parker, of accidentally using someone else's compass and living someone else's life. The best way to avoid this is to articulate clearly our own Workview and Lifeview, so we can build our own unique compass.

Our goal for your life is rather simple: *coherency.* A coherent life is one lived in such a way that you can clearly connect the dots between three things:

- **Who you are**
- **What you believe**
- **What you are doing**

For example, if in your Lifeview you believe in leaving the planet a better place for the next generation, and you work for a giant corporation that is polluting the planet (but for a really great salary), there is going to be a lack of coherency between what you believe and what you do—and as a result a lot of disappointment and discontent. Most of us have to make some trade-offs and compromises along the way, including some we may not like. If your Lifeview is that art is the only thing worth pursuing, and your Workview tells you that it's critical to make enough money so your kids have everything they need, you are going to make a compromise in your Lifeview while your children are dependent and at home. But that will be okay, because it's a conscious decision, which allows you to stay "on course" and coherent. Living coherently doesn't mean everything is in perfect order all the time. It simply means you are living in alignment with your values and have not sacrificed your integrity along the way. When you have a good compass guiding you, you have the power to cut these kinds of deals with yourself. If you can see the connections between who you are, what you believe, and what you are doing, you will know when you are on course, when there is tension, when there might need to be some careful compromises, and when you are in need of a major course correction. Our experience with our students has shown that the ability to connect these three dots increases your sense of self, and that helps you create more meaning in your life and have greater satisfaction.

So now it's time to build your compass and set out on your quest. Right now your quest is simple (and it's not to find the Holy Grail). Your quest is to design your life. We may all want the same things in life—a healthy and long life, work we enjoy and that matters, loving and meaningful relationships, and a hell of a lot of fun along the way—but how we think we'll get them is very different.

Workview Reflection

Write a short reflection about your Workview. We're not looking for a term paper here (and we're still not grading you), but we do want you really to write this down. Don't do it in your head. This should take about thirty minutes. Try to shoot for 250 words— less than a page of typed writing.

A Workview should address the critical issues related to what work is and what it means to you. It is not just a list of what you want from or out of work, but a general statement of your view of work. It's your definition for what good work deserves to be. A Workview may address such questions as:

- **Why work?**
- **What's work for?**
- **What does work mean?**
- **How does it relate to the individual, others, society?**
- **What defines good or worthwhile work?**
- **What does money have to do with it?**
- **What do experience, growth, and fulfillment have to do with it?**

In the years during which we've been helping people with this exercise, we've noticed that a Workview is a pretty new idea for most people. And we've noticed that when people get stuck on this exercise it is because they are just writing down what they're looking for in a job or an employment situation, which is a "job description." For this exercise, we're not interested in *what* work you want to do, but *why* you work.

What we're after is your philosophy of work—what it's for, what it means. This will essentially be your work manifesto. When using the term "work," we mean the broadest definition— not just what you do to make money or for "a job." Work is often the largest single component of most people's waking lives, and over a lifetime it occupies more of our attention and energy than anything else we do. Accordingly, we're suggesting you take the time to reflect and articulate what work and vocation mean to you (and perhaps what you hope work means for others as well).

Workviews can and do range widely in what they address and how they incorporate different issues, such as service to others and the world, money and standard of living, and growth, learning, skills, and talents. All of these can be part of the equation. We want you to address what you think is important. You do not have to address the question of service to others or any explicit connection to social issues. However, the positive psychologist Martin Seligman[1] found that the people who can make an explicit connection between their work and something socially meaningful to them are more likely to find satisfaction, and are better able to adapt to the inevitable stresses and compromises that come with working in the world. Since most people tell us they long for satisfying and meaningful work, we encourage you to explore the questions above and write down your Workview. Your compass won't be complete without it.

Lifeview Reflection

Just as you did with the Workview, please write a reflection on your Lifeview. This should also take no more than thirty minutes and be 250 words or so. Below are some questions often addressed in a Lifeview, just to get you started. The key thing is to write down whatever critical defining values and perspectives provide the basis for your understanding of life. Your Lifeview is what provides your definition of what have been called "matters of ultimate concern." It's what matters most to you.

- **Why are we here?**
- **What is the meaning or purpose of life?**
- **What is the relationship between the individual and others?**
- **Where do family, country, and the rest of the world fit in?**
- **What is good, and what is evil?**
- **Is there a higher power, God, or something transcendent, and if so, what impact does this have on your life?**
- **What is the role of joy, sorrow, justice, injustice, love, peace, and strife in life?**

We realize that these are somewhat philosophical questions, and we did just mention the "G" word. Some readers will see God as unimportant; others may have wanted us to address this up front as the most important issue. You've probably figured out by now that design is values-neutral, and we don't take sides. The questions, including the ones about God or spirituality, are given to provoke your thinking, and it's up to you to see which ones you want to try to answer. They are not talking points for religious or political debates, and there are no wrong answers—no wrong Lifeviews. The only way to do this incorrectly is not to do it at all. Besides that, be curious and think like a designer. Ask the questions that work for you, make up your own, and see what you discover.

Write down your answers.

Ready. Begin.

Coherency and Workview-Lifeview Integration

Read over your Workview and Lifeview, and write down a few thoughts on the following questions (please try to answer each of the questions):

* **Where do your views on work and life complement one another?**
* **Where do they clash?**
* **Does one drive the other? How?**

Please take some time to write up your thoughts on the integration of your two views. Our students tell us that this is where they often get the biggest "aha" moments, so please take this part of the exercise seriously and give the integration some thought. In most cases, this reflection will result in some editing of one or both of your views. By having your Workview and your Lifeview in harmony with each other, you increase your own clarity and ability to live a consciously coherent, meaningful life—one in which who you are, what you believe, and what you do are aligned. When you've got an accurate compass, you'll never stray off course for long.

True North

So now you have an articulated and integrated Lifeview and Workview. Ultimately, what these two views do is give you your "True North." They create your compass. They will help you know if you're on course or off course. At any moment you can assess where you are in relation to your True North. It's rare that people sail beautifully straight through their beautiful lives, always looking beautiful. In fact, as all sailors know, you can't chart a course of one straight line—you tack according to what the winds and the conditions allow. Heading True North, you may sail one way, then another direction, and then back the other way. Sometimes you sail close to the shoreline to avoid rough seas, adapting as needed. And sometimes storms hit and you get completely lost, or the entire sailboat tips over.

These are the times when it's best to have your Workview and your Lifeview handy to reorient yourself. Anytime you start to feel your life is not working, or you're going through a major transition, it's good to do a compass calibration. We do them at least once a year.

Rotate your tires.

Change the battery in your smoke detector.

Double-check your Workview and Lifeview and make sure they align.

Anytime you're changing your situation, or pursuing a new thing, or wondering what you're doing at a particular job—stop. Before you start, it's a good idea to check your compass and orient yourself. Now that you have your compass, it's time to "find your way."

This is a quest, after all.

Dysfunctional Belief: *I should know where I'm going!*
Reframe: *I won't always know where I'm going—but I can always know whether I'm going in the right direction.*

Try Stuff

Workview and Lifeview

1. Write a short reflection about your Workview. This should take about thirty minutes. Shoot for about 250 words—less than a page of typed writing.

2. Write a short reflection about your Lifeview. This should also take no more than thirty minutes and be 250 words or so.

3. Read over your Lifeview and Workview, and answer each of these questions:

   a. Where do your views on work and life complement one another?

   b. Where do they clash?

   c. Does one drive the other? How?

3

Wayfinding

Michael was happy. A popular boy living in a small college town in central California, he played sports, hung out with his friends, and enjoyed the fairly carefree life that comes with being a popular boy who plays sports and hangs out with his friends. Michael didn't spend a whole lot of time thinking about or planning for the future. He just did whatever was in front of him, and life seemed to work out fine. His mother, however, had plans. Lots of plans. She planned for Michael to go to college, chose where he would apply, and even chose what he would major in. This resulted in Michael's attending Cal Poly in San Luis Obispo and majoring in civil engineering. Michael wasn't particularly invested in being a civil engineer; he was simply following Mom's plan.

He did fine in his major and graduated from college. Michael then fell in love with Skylar, who was finishing her degree and moving to Amsterdam to take a corporate consulting job. Michael followed Skylar and took a perfectly good civil-engineering position in Amsterdam, where he did a decent job. Michael was again happily following a path in life that had been chosen for him, and not once having stopped to consider what he wanted to do or who he wanted to become. He had never articulated his Lifeview or Workview, and had always let other people steer his course and determine his direction. It had worked well enough so far.

After Amsterdam, Michael traveled back to California with Skylar (now his wife), who found a great job she loved; Michael took a job in a nearby civil-engineering firm. That's when the trouble began. He was doing all the things respectable civil engineers do—but he was bored, restless, and miserable. His new-found misery left him confused. He had no idea where to go or what to do. For the first time in his life, his plan wasn't working, and, without a direction, Michael felt absolutely lost.

Dysfunctional Belief: *Work is not supposed to be enjoyable; that's why they call it work.*
Reframe: *Enjoyment is a guide to finding the right work for you.*

Lots of people had advice for Michael. A few friends suggested he start his own civil-engineering practice, believing that his problem was due to his working for someone else. His father-in-law told him, "You're a smart guy. You're an engineer, so you know your math. You should be in finance. You should be a stockbroker." Michael thought about all the many suggestions and started calculating how he could quit his job and go back to school to study finance, or maybe go to business school. He considered all of these options because, frankly, he wasn't sure what the problem was. Had he failed as a civil engineer? Had civil engineering failed him? Was he just supposed to put up with it? After all, it was only a job, right?

Wrong.

Finding Your Way

Wayfinding is the ancient art of figuring out where you are going when you don't actually know your destination. For wayfinding, you need a compass and you need a direction. Not a map—a direction. Think of the American explorers Lewis and Clark. They didn't have a map when Jefferson sent them out to travel through the land acquired in the Louisiana Purchase and make their way to the Pacific. While wayfinding to the ocean, they mapped the route (140 maps, to be exact). Wayfinding your life is similar. Since there's no *one* destination in life, you can't put your goal into your GPS and get the turn-by-turn directions for how to get there. What you can do is pay attention to the clues in front of you, and make your best way forward with the tools you have at hand. We think the first clues are *engagement* and *energy*.

Engagement

Civil engineering hadn't failed Michael. He just wasn't paying attention to his life, and all he knew was that something wasn't working. At thirty-four years old, Michael didn't know what he liked and what he didn't like. When he came to us for help, he was on the verge of upending his life and career completely, and for no good reasons. We had him spend a few weeks doing a simple logging assignment at the end of every workday. Michael wrote down when during the day he had been feeling bored, restless, or unhappy at his job, and what exactly he had been doing during those times (the times when he was *disengaged*). He also wrote down when he was excited, focused, and having a good time at work, and what exactly he was doing during those times (the times when he was *engaged*). Michael was working on what we call the Good Time Journal.

Why did we have Michael do this (and, yes, we're going to ask you to do it, too)? Because we were trying to get him to catch himself in the act of having a good time. When you learn what activities reliably engage you, you're discovering and articulating something that can be very helpful in your life design work. Remember that designers have a bias to action—which is just another way of saying that we pay a lot of attention to doing things, and not just to thinking about things. Logging when you are and aren't engaged and energized will help you pay attention to what you're doing and discover what's working.

Flow: Total Engagement

Flow is engagement on steroids. Flow is that state of being in which time stands still, you're totally engaged in an activity, and the challenge of that particular activity matches up with your skill—so you're neither bored because it's too easy nor anxious because it's too hard. People describe this state of engagement as "euphoric," "in the zone," and "freakin' awesome." Flow was "discovered" by Professor Mihaly Csikszentmihalyi, who has been researching this phenomenon since the 1970s. When he first described the state of flow, he had studied the detailed activities of thousands of people going about their daily lives and was able to isolate this very special form of intense engagement.[1]

People in flow report the experience as having these sorts of attributes:

- **Experiencing complete involvement in the activity.**
- **Feeling a sense of ecstasy or euphoria.**
- **Having great inner clarity — knowing just what to do and how to do it.**
- **Being totally calm and at peace.**
- **Feeling as if time were standing still — or disappearing in an instant.**

Flow can happen during almost any physical or mental activity, and often when both are combined. Dave goes into flow while editing minute details in a class lesson plan, or out on his sailboat, trimming the sails as it heels into a rising wind. Bill admits to being a flow junkie and finds advising students, sketching in his idea log, or chopping an onion with his favorite knife to be moments most conducive to flow. Flow is one of those "hard to describe but you know it when you feel it" qualitative experiences that you'll have to identify for yourself. As the ultimate state of personal engagement, flow experiences have a special place in designing your life, so it's important to get good at capturing them in your Good Time Journal.

Flow is play for grown-ups. In the life design dashboard, we assessed our health, work, play, and love. The element we all find the most elusive in our busy modern lives is "play." You might think that we all have too many responsibilities to have much time for play. Sure, we can strive to have our work and our chores engage skills we like using, but face it—it's work, not play. Maybe. Maybe not. Flow is one key to what we call adult play, and a really rewarding and satisfying career involves a lot of flow states. The essence of play is being fully immersed and joyful in what you're doing, without being constantly distracted by concerns about the outcomes. When we're in flow, that's exactly what's going on—we are fully present to what we're doing, so present we don't even notice time. Seen this way, flow is something we should strive to make a regular part of our work life (and home life, and exercise life, and love life . . . you get the idea).

Energy

After engagement, the second wayfinding clue to look for is energy. Human beings, like all living things, need energy to live and to thrive. Men and women used to spend most of their daily energy on physical tasks. For most of human history, men and women were working at hunting and gathering, raising children, and raising crops, most of their time consumed with energy-intensive physical labor.

Nowadays, many of us are knowledge workers, and we use our brains to do the heavy lifting. The brain is a very energy-hungry organ. Of the roughly two thousand calories we consume a day, five hundred go to running our brains. That's astonishing: the brain represents only about 2 percent of our body weight, and yet it takes up 25 percent of the energy we consume every day. It's no wonder that the way we *invest our attention* is critical to whether or not we feel high or low energy.[2]

We engage in physical and mental activities all day long. Some activities sustain our energy and some drain it; we want to track those energy flows as part of our Good Time Journal exercise. Once you have a good handle on where your energy goes every week, you can start redesigning your activities to maximize your vitality. Remember, life design is about getting more out of your current life—and not only about redesigning a whole new life. Even if questions about some big change in your life may be what brought you to this book, most life design work is directed at tuning up and improving the life you're in, without having to make huge structural changes like changing jobs or moving or going back to grad school.

You may be wondering, "Isn't tracking my energy level kind of the same thing as tracking how engaged I am?" Yes and no. Yes, high levels of engagement often coincide with high levels of energy, but not necessarily. A colleague of Dave's, a brilliantly fast-thinking computer engineer, found arguing for his point of view an engaging activity, because it made him think on his feet. He was great at it, and often found other people at work asking him to make their arguments for them. But he noticed that getting into those arguments totally exhausted him, even when he "won." He was not a contentious person, and though it seemed fun at the time to outwit others, he always felt terrible when it was over. Energy is also unique in that it can go negative—some activities can actually suck the life right out of us and send us drained into whatever comes next. Boredom is a big energy-suck, but it's much easier to recover from boredom than from being de-energized, so it's important to pay specific attention to your energy levels.

It's About Joy

After working on his Good Time Journal and paying attention to when he was engaged, when he was in flow, and what was energizing for him, Michael realized that he loved his job as a civil engineer when he was working on difficult and complex engineering problems. The times that drained him and made him miserable were those when he was dealing with difficult personalities, struggling to communicate with others, and performing other administrative tasks and distractions that had nothing to do with the intricate task of engineering.

The end result was that, for the first time in his life, Michael was paying detailed attention to what really worked for him. The results were amazing. By simply discovering when he was enjoying himself at work and what caused his energies to rise and fall, Michael discovered that he actually enjoyed civil engineering. It was the people stuff, the proposal writing, and the fee negotiations that he hated. He just had to find a way to craft his job so that he was doing more of what he loved and less of what he hated. Instead of business school (which would probably have been a disaster, and an expensive one at that), Michael decided to double down on engineering. He ended up entering a Ph.D. program and is now a high-level civil and structural engineer, who spends his time, mostly alone, working on the kind of complex engineering problems that make him really happy. And he's become so technically valuable that no one asks him to do the administrative stuff anymore. On good days, he goes home with more energy than when he left for work in the morning. And that's a pretty great way to work.

Here's another key element when you're wayfinding in life: follow the joy; follow what engages and excites you, what brings you alive. Most people are taught that work is always hard and that we have to suffer through it. Well, there are parts of any job or any career that are hard and annoying—but if most of what you do at work is not bringing you alive, then it's killing you. It's your career, after all, and you are going to be spending a lot of time doing it—we calculate it at 90,000 to 125,000 hours during the course of your lifetime. If it's not fun, a lot of your life is going to suck.

Now, what makes work fun? It's not what you might think. It's not one unending office party. It's not getting paid a lot of money. It's not having multiple weeks of paid vacations. Work is fun when you are actually leaning into your strengths and are deeply engaged and energized by what you're doing.

What About Purpose?

At about this stage, we're often asked, "Well, this is all great, but where do purpose and mission come into it? There's more to life than just being engaged and energized. I want to be doing work I care about, work that's important to me and that matters."

We couldn't agree more. That's why we addressed building your compass (your well-integrated Workview and Lifeview) in chapter 2. As we suggested, it's crucial for you to assess how well your work fits your values and priorities—how *coherent* your work is with who you are and what you believe. We are not suggesting a life singularly focused on engagement and energy level. We are suggesting that focused attention on engagement and energy level can provide very helpful clues to wayfinding your path forward. Life design consists of a whole set of ideas and tools that work together flexibly. We'll give you lots of suggestions, but in the end you'll decide which things to focus on and how to organize your life design project. Now let's get started on your Good Time Journal.

Good Time Journal Exercise

We're going to ask you to do a Good Time Journal, as Michael did. Just how you build yours is up to you. You can make your entries all by hand in a bound journal, or use a three-ring binder with loose sheets, or even do it on your computer (though we strongly recommend you try it by hand, so you can sketch in your journal or binder). The most important thing is that you actually do it and regularly make entries; whatever format you will most enjoy and will use most often is the way to go.

There are two elements to the Good Time Journal:

- **Activity Log (where I record where I'm engaged and energized)**
- **Reflections (where I discover what I am learning)**

The Activity Log simply lists your primary activities and how engaged ⓕ and energized ⓔ you were by those activities. We recommend that you make Activity Log entries daily, to be sure to capture lots of good information. If every few days is easier, that's fine as well, but log activities at least twice a week or you'll miss too much. If you're using a binder, you can make log sheets using the worksheet at the end of this chapter, which has little gauges for how engaged ⓕ and energized ⓔ you are by your activities (or download it at www.designingyour.life). You can also just draw gauges (or whatever engagement and energy symbols you like) into your journal book. Do what works for you—just get the information down on paper.

All of us are motivated by different kinds of work activities. Your job is to figure out which ones motivate you—with as much specificity as you can. It will take a while to get the hang of this, because, if you're like most people, you've not been paying detailed attention to this sort of thing. Sure, there are times when we all come home at the end of the day and say, "That was *great*," or "That *sucked*," but we seldom sift through the particulars of what contributed to those experiences. A day is made up of many moments, some of which are great, some of which suck, and most of which lie somewhere in between. Your job is to drill down into the particulars of your day and catch yourself in the act of having a good time.

The second element of the Good Time Journal is reflection, looking over your Activity Log and noticing trends, insights, surprises—anything that is a clue to what does and doesn't work for you. We recommend doing your Activity Log for at least three weeks, or whatever period of time you need to be sure you capture all the various kinds of activities that arise in your current situation (some activities may only come around every few weeks). Then we recommend that you do your Good Time Journal reflection weekly, so your reflections are based on more than just a single experience of each activity.

Write your weekly reflections on blank pages in your Good Time Journal.

We've included a page from one of Bill's recent Good Time Journal Activity Logs.

Bill's reflection included these observations:

He noticed that his drawing class and office hours reliably created flow states, and that teaching and "date night" were the activities that returned significantly more energy than they consumed. Doubling up on those activities would certainly be one way to energize his week. His weekly faculty meeting is sometimes full of interesting conversations and sometimes not, so he drew two arrows on his energy diagram. He was not surprised that budget meetings sucked energy out of his day—he's never liked the fiscal side of things much (though he appreciates that they're crucial).

Bill adjusted his schedule to surround these less engaging activities with more engaging activities, and to give himself small rewards when he completes "energy-negative" tasks. The best way to deal with these energy-negative activities is to make sure that you are well rested and have the energy reserves needed to "do them right." Otherwise, you might find yourself doing them again—costing you more energy than they should.

Bill was surprised that coaching master's students, the students he likes and spends the most time with, was such a drain on his week. After journaling a bit on that subject, he discovered two things: (1) he was trying to coach in a bad environment (the

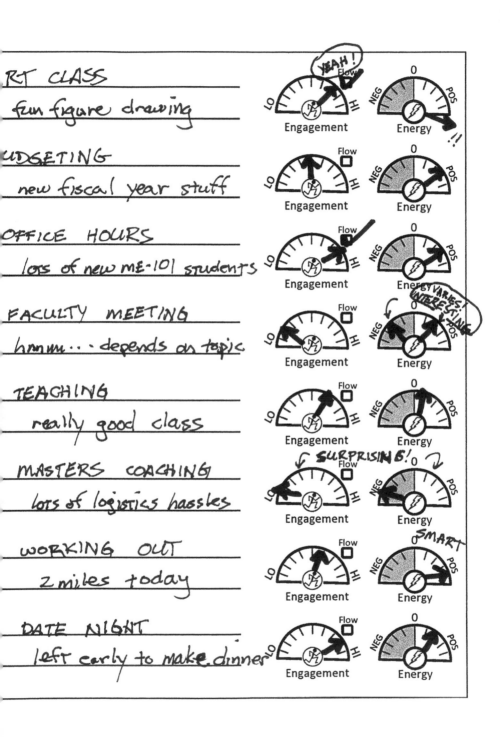

noisy graduate studio) and (2) his coaching interaction wasn't effective—his students weren't "getting it." Those two observations resulted in a redesign of his Tuesday-night class environment (he changed classrooms) and a shift in the coaching structure from meeting one to one with each student to coaching in small groups, so students could help one another during the interactions. These changes worked so well that a few weeks later he was regularly going into flow during coaching sessions. The budgeting still sucked, of course, but it's not that big a part of the job, and the new coaching flow moments help make it more bearable.

Bill was using his Good Time Journal primarily to improve his current life design. Michael did the exercise in search of what strategic career path to take. They had very different goals and got very different results, but both used exactly the same technique—paying detailed attention to what was engaging and energizing them.

Zooming In— Getting to the Good Stuff

After a week or two, when you've got a decent body of entries in your Good Time Journal and you're starting to notice some interesting things, it's time to zoom in and take the exercise to the next level. Typically, after you start to get the hang of paying more detailed attention to your days, you notice that some of your log entries could be more specific: you need to zoom in to see more clearly. The idea is to try to become as precise as possible; the clearer you are on what is and isn't working for you, the better you can set your wayfinding direction. For instance . . . What you initially logged as "Staff Mtg—Enjoyed it for once today!" might, after you've looked at it again, be more accurately restated as "Staff Mtg—Felt great when I rephrased what Jon said and everyone went 'Ooooh—exactly!'" This more precise version tells a much more useful story about what specific activity or behavior engages you. And it opens the door to developing even greater self-awareness. When your entries have that kind of detail in them, your reflections can be more insightful. When journaling your reflection on the log entry about that staff meeting, you might ask yourself, "Was I more engaged by *artfully rephrasing* Jon's comment (getting the articulation dialed in just right) or by *facilitating consensus* among the staff (being the guy who made the group's 'Now we get it!' unifying moment happen)?" If you conclude that artful articulation was the real sweet spot of that staff meeting moment for you, that important insight can help you be on the lookout for content-creation opportunities over group facilitation opportunities. Take this sort of observation and reflection as far as you find helpful (and no further—you don't want to get stuck in your journal).

AEIOU

Getting great insights out of your Good Time Journal reflections isn't always easy, so here's a tool designers use to make detailed and accurate observations—part of getting good at the curiosity mind-set. It's the AEIOU method[3] that provides you five sets of questions you can use when reflecting on your Activity Log.

Activities. What were you actually doing? Was this a structured or an unstructured activity? Did you have a specific role to play (team leader) or were you just a participant (at the meeting)?

Environments. Our environment has a profound effect on our emotional state. You feel one way at a football stadium, another in a cathedral. Notice where you were when you were involved in the activity. What kind of a place was it, and how did it make you feel?

Interactions. What were you interacting with—people or machines? Was it a new kind of interaction or one you are familiar with? Was it formal or informal?

Objects. Were you interacting with any objects or devices— iPads or smartphones, hockey sticks or sailboats? What were the objects that created or supported your feeling engaged?

Users. Who else was there, and what role did they play in making it either a positive or a negative experience?

Using AEIOU can really help you to zoom in effectively and discover specifically what it is that is or isn't working for you. Here are two examples:

Lydia is a contract writer. She works to help experts document their procedures in manuals. And she'd come to conclude that she hated working with people—mostly because of how awful she felt after going to meetings, and how great she felt when she got to write all day. She was wondering how she could make a living without ever going to a meeting again when she did the Good Time Journal and used the AEIOU method. When she zoomed in, she observed that she actually liked people fine—when she got to meet with only one or two of them and either work hard on the writing or do rapid brainstorming on new project ideas (activity). She hated meetings about planning, schedules, and business strategy and any meeting with more than six people in it; she just couldn't track all the different points of view (environment). She realized that she was just an intense and focused worker, and that her intensity could be either nurtured or frustrated by other people (users), depending on the form of collaboration (interactions).

Basra simply loved higher education. It didn't matter what she was doing—if she was doing it on a university campus, she was a happy camper (environment). So she went to work at the university where she had done her undergraduate degree. For five or six years, she was very happy doing anything and everything from fund-raising to new student orientation (activity). Then it all began to fade, and she was nervous that her love affair with education was over. She did a version of the Good Time Journal and realized that she still loved the university, but had gotten into the wrong job. As she approached her thirties, environment alone was not enough; role mattered now. She'd accepted a promotion that transferred her from student affairs—and lots of interesting student interactions—to legal affairs—and lots of meetings with administrators and lawyers (users), and paperwork (objects). She figured it out and took a slight demotion to accept a position in the housing office, where she once again could have interactions of a more constructive nature and less paperwork.

As you work on your reflections in the Good Time Journal, try using this AEIOU method to get more out of your observations. It is important to record whatever comes up and not to judge yourself—there are no right or wrong feelings about your experience. The thing to focus on is that this kind of information is going to be incredibly helpful in designing your life.

Mining the Mountaintop

Your past is waiting to be mined for insights, too—especially your mountaintop moments, or "peak experiences." Peak experiences in our past—even our long-ago past—can be telling. Take some time to reflect on your memories of past peak work-related experiences and do a Good Time Journal Activity Log and reflection on them to see what you find. Those memories have stuck with you for good reason. You can make a list of those peak experiences, or write them out as a narrative or story. It can be very enjoyable to set to words the story of that great time when you were on the team that planned what they're still calling the Ultimate Sales Meeting, or when you wrote the procedure manual that they still pass out to new writers as the standard for doing it right. Having the narrative of your peak experiences written down will make it easier to extract from those stories the activities that most engaged and energized you, and to discover insights that you can apply today.

Using past experience is particularly useful if you aren't currently in a situation that lends itself to a successful Good Time Journal exercise, such as if you're between jobs. It's also helpful if you're just getting started on your professional life and don't yet have much experience. If so, think about activities that you did in other areas of your life (perhaps even decades ago) when you felt that life was working. A historical Good Time Journal on past projects from school, summer programs, volunteer projects— anything that you were seriously engaged by—can be useful. When looking back, do beware of revisionist history—being too kind to the good days or too critical of the bad times. Just try to be honest.

Enjoy the Journey

This new way of noticing will help guide you in finding what's next for you. Like Lewis and Clark, you are starting to map some of the territory you've already covered, and are starting to see new possibilities in the territory ahead. You are moving from one level of awareness to another, really exploring how things make you (not your mom, dad, boss, or spouse) feel. You have started to wayfind—moving from where you are to the next possible place. Armed with your compass and your Good Time Journal insights, you can do a great job of wayfinding.

Michael found his way.

Lewis and Clark found their way.

You can find your way as well.

The next step is to generate as many options as possible, so you have lots to experiment with and prototype.

For that, we're going to need to do a little mind mapping.

Try Stuff
Good Time Journal

1. Complete a log of your daily activities, using the worksheet provided (or in your own notebook). Note when you are engaged and/or energized and what you are doing during those times. Try to do this daily, or at the very least every few days.

2. Continue this daily logging for three weeks.

3. At the end of each week, jot down your reflections—notice which activities are engaging and energizing, and which ones are not.

4. Are there any surprises in your reflections?

5. Zoom in and try to get even more specific about what does or does not engage and energize you.

6. Use the AEIOU method as needed to help you in your reflections.

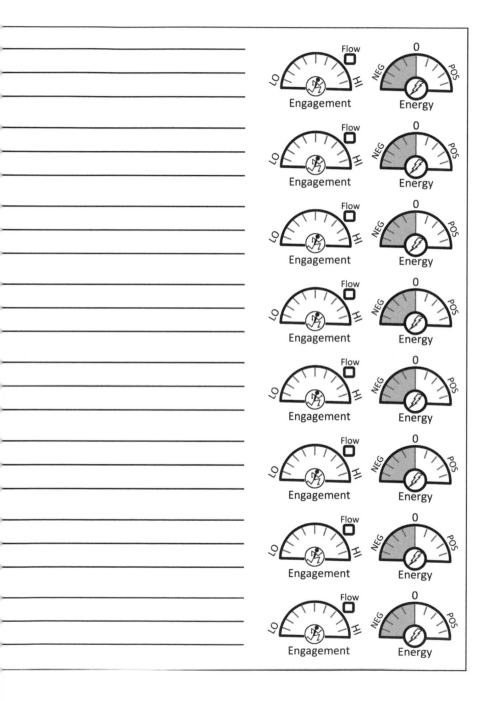

4

Getting Unstuck

Grant was stuck. He worked for a major car-rental company, and after doing his Good Time Journal, he realized he was spending the majority of his days in activities that neither engaged nor energized him. He hated dealing with irate customers. He didn't like completing endless boilerplate contracts. He hated reciting the same exact script every day. He didn't like having to up-sell customers constantly. But most of all he hated feeling as if he didn't matter. He didn't want to be a small, unimportant cog in a giant corporate machine. Grant wanted to work someplace where he could leave his mark. He wanted to have influence. He wanted what he did to be important to someone. Anyone.

Grant didn't completely hate his job, but he couldn't think of a single time when he had ever experienced anything close to a state of flow. Work equaled a kind of dull misery. He watched the clock. He waited for his paycheck each week. And the weekends couldn't come soon enough or last long enough. The only time he liked what he was doing was when he was hiking among the redwoods, or playing a pickup basketball game with his friends, or helping his niece and nephew with their homework.

None of which would pay the bills.

Grant was about to be promoted to store manager, and this made him feel more stuck than ever. He had never dreamed of working for a car-rental agency, but, no matter how long and hard he thought about it, he couldn't come up with a realistic idea for a different career. He had no idea where to begin, even. Sure, he would love to be a rock star, or a major-league baseball player. But he didn't sing or play an instrument, and he had bailed out of Little League at the age of twelve. A literature major in college, he had taken the first job that paid more than minimum wage. And now he was trapped. Grant didn't want to resign himself to renting cars for the rest of his life, but he felt there were no other options. "Some guys are just unlucky," he thought. "Some guys just aren't meant to leave their mark."

Grant felt defeated because he thought that all he could do was what he'd always done—and because he wasn't thinking like a designer. Designers know that you never go with your first idea. Designers know that when you choose from lots of options you choose better. Many people are like Grant: they get stuck trying to make their first idea work.

Grant needed to start thinking like a designer.

Dysfunctional Belief: *I'm stuck.*
Reframe: *I'm never stuck, because I can always generate a lot of ideas.*

Sharon is a paralegal who worked at a prestigious law firm in Boston until she was laid off. Now she spends six hours a day on the

Internet, looking for a job. She's been doing this for over a year. She's completely demoralized; any shred of self-confidence evaporated long ago. In fact, being a paralegal wasn't her goal in the first place—it was her backup plan. She went to business school, but the economy was in the dumpster when she graduated in 2009. She could not find a job as a marketing executive, which she had been told was the "right thing" to do with an M.B.A. Like so many, she thought that doing the "right thing" would make her happy. But Sharon wasn't remotely close to happy. The truth is that Sharon had no idea what she really *wanted* out of business school, and this lack of genuine interest was probably apparent to the people who interviewed her. She had spent a long time trying to do the right thing instead of doing what was right for Sharon. A year into her job search, she felt she was out of options. She felt defeated. But Sharon wasn't really out of options—she just hadn't come up with a lot of real options in the first place.

Dysfunctional Belief: *I have to find the one right idea.*
Reframe: *I need a lot of ideas so that I can explore any number of possibilities for my future.*

With no idea other than to keep on doing what she was doing, Sharon, like Grant, was stuck.

Most people do the same thing Sharon did when they need work: they look at the job listings and look for a job that they think they can get. This is one of the worst ways to get a job, and actually has the lowest success rate (we'll discuss the phenomenon in detail in chapter 7). This way of thinking is not design thinking; it's just grasping whatever might be in reach, and it's unlikely to result in long-term satisfaction. If the kids are hungry, the bank is about to foreclose on your house, or you owe a guy named Louie a lot of money, then by all means take whatever job you can get. But when the wolf has backed off a bit, it's time to wayfind to jobs you might actually want. And don't worry about being stuck. Designers get stuck all the time. Being stuck can be a launching pad for creativity. When you think like a designer, you know how to ideate—how to "flare"—to come up with lots of options for lots of possible futures.

Look, it's simple. You can't know what you want until you know what you *might* want, so you are going to have to generate a lot of ideas and possibilities.

Accept the problem.

Get stuck.

Get over it, and ideate, ideate, ideate!

Ideate This

We're going to ask you to get out of the box of being realistic and venture into the wide world of "what I might want." It's time to embrace being stuck. Grant was stuck. Sharon was stuck. We're all stuck in some way in some areas of our lives. That's where we need ideation, which is a fancy word for coming up with lots of ideas. Wild ideas. Crazy ideas. We're going to teach you how to have more ideas than you ever thought possible. So many people get stuck chasing their first idea, or the perfect idea, or that one big idea that will solve the problem, will be the answer, and will dig them out of whatever hole they are currently stuck in. That's a lot of pressure. Believing that there's only one idea out there leads to a lot of pressure and indecision.

"I'm just not sure."

"I don't want to blow it."

"I really need to get this right."

"If I just had a better (the right, a killer) idea, then all would be well."

Let's stop right here, so we can be the first to tell you an amazing fact: All will be well.

It will.

Those of us fortunate enough to live in the modern world with access to some degree of choice, freedom, mobility, education, and technology spend most of our time immersed in a world obsessed with optimization. There's always got to be a better idea, a better way—even a best way. That kind of thinking is pretty dangerous to life design. The truth is that all of us have more than one life in us. When we ask our students, "How many lifetimes' worth of living are there in you?," the average answer is 3.4. And if you accept this idea—that there are multiple great designs for your life, though you'll still only get to live one—it is rather liberating. There is no one idea for your life. There are many lives you could live happily and productively (no matter how many years old you are), and there are lots of different paths you could take to live each of those productive, amazingly different lives. So do the math; this adds up to tons of different possible ideas you might have. And we're going to give you the tools to generate such ideas.

Quantity has a quality all its own. In life design, more is better, because more ideas equal access to better ideas, and better ideas lead to a better design. Expanding your thinking improves your ability to ideate and allows for more innovation. If you work through lots of ideas, your chances of hitting on some that can be really energizing for you go up, which increases your chance of creating something that can work and that you'll love. More ideas also equal new insights.

Designers love to ideate broadly and wildly. They love the crazy ideas as much as or more than the sensible ones. Why? Most people think that designers are just "out there" and prefer crazy stuff because they're edgy, avant-garde, dark-sunglass-wearing kinds of people (think berets, cool shoes, and the hippest restaurants). That may be true, but it's not the point. Designers learn to have lots of wild ideas because they know that the number one enemy of creativity is judgment. Our brains are so tightly wired to be critical, find problems, and leap to judgment that it's a wonder any ideas ever make it out! We have to defer judgment and silence the inner critic if we want to get *all* our ideas out. If we don't, we may have a few good ideas, but the majority will have been lost—silently imprisoned behind the wall of judgment our prefrontal cortex has erected to safeguard us from making mistakes or looking foolish. Now, we love the prefrontal cortex and wouldn't be caught in public without it, but we don't want it taking our ideas hostage prematurely. If we can get out into the wild idea space, then we know we've overcome premature judgment. The crazy ideas may not be the ones we pick (and rarely are, actually), but often after having the crazy ideas, we have moved to a new creative space, and we can see new and innovative possibilities that can work.

So let's bring on the crazy.

Usually our students find this part of the process to be the most exciting, engaging, and just plain fun. Who doesn't like to generate a lot of great and crazy ideas? You may or may not think that you are a creative person, but that doesn't matter. Remember our motto "You Are Here," and get ready to work with whatever level of personal creativity you think you have. We'll build from there. Our goal is to energize and expand on your capacity for generating lots and lots of solutions to the myriad problems that come up when you are designing your life.

As a life designer, you need to embrace two philosophies:

1. **You choose better when you have lots of good ideas to choose from.**
2. **You never choose your first solution to any problem.**

Our minds are generally lazy and like to get rid of problems as quickly as possible, so they surround first ideas with a lot of positive chemicals to make us "fall in love" with them. Do not fall in love with your first idea. This relationship almost never works out. Most often, our first solutions are pretty average and not very creative. Humans have a tendency to suggest the obvious first. Learning to use great ideation tools helps you overcome this bias toward the obvious and helps you regain a sense of creative confidence.

Even those of you who might think that you are not creative can probably remember back to a time when you didn't feel this way. Perhaps it was in kindergarten, or first or second grade, when singing, dancing, and drawing seemed like natural forms of self-expression. You were not self-conscious, nor were you judging whether your drawings were art, or your singing professional, or your dancing worthy of others' attention. You felt free to create any natural form of your own self-expression without limits.

You can probably also remember, typically in vivid detail, a time when a teacher said, "You're not an artist, you can't draw," or a classmate said, "You dance funny," or some other adult said, "Stop singing, you're ruining the song for everyone." Ouch! We're sorry if this creativity-killing moment happened to you. And the creativity-killing moments kept happening in middle school and high school, where social norms took the place of scolding adults, and we learned to rein in our differences for fear of being called out. It's a wonder that any shred of our personal creativity survives as we grow up.

But trust us, it's in there. We're going to help you discover it.

Mind Mapping

The first ideation technique we're going to teach you is called mind mapping. It's a great tool for ideating by yourself, and a great method for getting unstuck. Mind mapping works by using simple free association of words, one after another, to open up the idea space and come up with new solutions. The graphical nature of the method allows ideas and their associations to be captured automatically. This technique teaches you to generate lots of ideas, and because it is a visual method, it bypasses your inner logical/verbal censor.

The mind-mapping process has three steps:

1. **Picking a topic**
2. **Making the mind map**

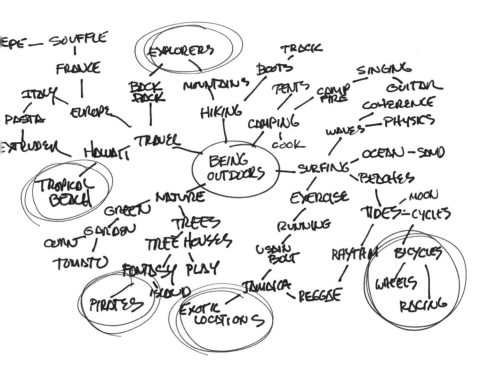

3. **Making secondary connections and creating concepts (mashing it all up)**

The image above is of Grant's mind map, which he made while being stuck on the problem of how to find the "perfect" job. You'll remember that when Grant looked over his Good Time Journal the only positive experiences he could find had something to do with hiking in the redwoods near his house. So he decided to mind-map around that. You can see he put BEING OUTDOORS in the center of his mind map and drew a circle around it. This is step one.

Step two is making the mind map. For this, you take the original idea and write down five or six things related to that idea. Be rigorous in writing down the first words that come to mind. Now repeat this process with the words in the second ring. Draw three or four lines from each word, and free-associate new words related to these prompts. The words that come up for you do not need to be associated to the words or question in the center, only the word in the second ring. Repeat this process until you have at least three or four rings of word associations.

In Grant's example, he wrote down travel, hiking, surfing, camping, and nature. These things are all related directly to his idea of BEING OUTDOORS. He then took each of those words and created new branches of word associations. Hiking reminded Grant of mountains, which led to explorers. Travel led him to Hawaii, Europe, and backpacking, and Hawaii led him to tropical beaches. France, an association with Europe, took him to crêpes, which took him to Nutella, which, though interesting, turned out to be a dead end. But surfing led to beaches, which led to tides, which led to cycles, bicycles, and racing. It also led to Jamaica, then through Usain Bolt (Grant's brain turns out to be more creative than he thought), and on to the idea of exotic locations.

This whole process of creating layers and word associations took three to five minutes; you want to give yourself a time limit so you do this fast and bypass your inner censor. The next step is to take this random association of words and highlight a few things that might be interesting (or that jump out at you) and mash them together into a few concepts. You want to pick from the very outer layer or perimeter of the mind map, because that is the stuff that is two or three steps away from your conscious thinking. Even though being outdoors eventually took Grant to bicycle racing and Usain Bolt, in Grant's hidden unconscious these are all linked back to his original prompt. Grant pulled out the random words that seemed interesting—in this case, explorers, tropical beaches, pirates, kids, exotic locations, and bicycle racing. Then he took these individual components and mashed them up into a couple of possible ideas.

Could he work part-time at an Explorer Camp for kids who liked the outdoors? Better yet, make it a Pirate Camp and have it at a beach? How about accepting the promotion he was offered, but only if they let him move to a rental office near a beach (he looked it up and found that his company had an office in Santa Cruz, California—yes!)? Or, even better, someplace really exotic, like Hawaii, where he could coach at a Pirate Surf Camp for kids (turns out his company had an office there, too). And maybe, if he accepted the promotion, he'd make enough money to afford a four-day workweek so that he'd have some time to "explore" some of these new ideas.

This is innovation.

Grant is no longer stuck. In fact, he has more good ideas than he knows what to do with. And, more important, he's starting to think that it's not about finding the perfect job, it's about making the job he has "perfect." It turns out it pays to work for a multinational car-rental company with offices all over the world. Doing his mind map made Grant realize that he has more to work with than he thought, and he can use his current job as the springboard to what's next.

It's important to remember when you do this not to censor your words. That's why we suggest you do it fast. Just write down the first words that come to mind. If you censor yourself, you limit your potential for generating new and novel ideas. David Kelley, the founder of the d.school, says you often have to go through the wild ideas to get to the actionable good ideas. So don't be afraid to come up with crazy stuff. It may be the jumping-off point for something really practical and really new. Also, you should create your mind map on a big piece of paper. You are looking for lots of ideas—so make your map as graphic and as big as possible. Go out and get a giant piece of butcher paper or a large white board, and have big ideas.

The bigger the better.

Stuck on Steroids: Anchor Problems

There's a certain class of problems—the ones that just won't go away—that we call anchor problems. Like a physical anchor, they hold us in one place and prevent motion. They keep us stuck, much as Grant and Sharon were stuck with their career problems. If we are going to practice good life design, it is important to notice when we are stuck with an anchor problem.

Dave found himself with an anchor problem, but it didn't have to do with his career, like Grant and Sharon; this problem hit closer to home. You see, Dave is a shop kind of guy—as in "workshop." His dad (Dave the Third) was an incredible craftsman and had an amazing shop, so of course Dave had to have a cool shop, too. But Dave is less craftsman and more fix-it guy, so he didn't need quite the same shop layout as his dad. This means that, with careful planning and maintenance, Dave has been able to achieve the all-time garage twofer—a killer shop that still allows room to park the cars inside.

Don't judge Dave's dreams.

He loved it and vowed he'd have that kind of garage the rest of his life. And then he moved to the beach. And in that move he found out he had a fifth of his former storage space to fit his stuff in. And he found himself with an anchor problem, an anchor problem that's lasted years.

For the first few years, Dave had to rent three storage units in addition to filling the garage at the beach. One by one, year after year, he got rid of the storage units, but the last car-evicting pile of junk has never been cleared from the garage. And as far as getting the shop properly laid out . . . well, don't ask. He's lived with the All-American Garage Disaster for over five years now, and of course he's gotten too used to it. Every summer for four years, he's vowed to clean it out and get the shop set up, but he's been overwhelmed every time. Though he's got a vision of his old, near-perfect garage layout, he fears he'll just never get there. He begins in earnest, removing the first layer of old bike parts and VHS tapes, but then he gets discouraged at the looming pile, and distracts himself with something more doable—like replacing the alternator in the truck. Fix-it guy strikes again. Then it's Christmas, with all those boxes down from the attic, and . . . fuhgedaboudit.

Dave is anchored on this problem because he's anchored to the one and only solution he's been willing to accept—a perfect cars-plus-workshop layout. It's such a huge job now, Dave doesn't even try, so everybody gets to slalom through the obstacle course of the garage while the ocean sun and salt air fade the paint on the cars parked outside.

The only way Dave can get unanchored from this immovable situation is to reframe his solution and prototype a little. He could:

1.   **Reframe so that the goal is just a workbench and inside storage for bikes and camping gear.**
2.   **Reframe so that he still needs just one small storage unit (for life), and buy back his garage for about a hundred dollars a month.**
3.   **Be mindful of process and break it into smaller projects: (a) give away old books and music, (b) reduce to only four bikes, (c) clear the floor of boxes, (d) clear the workbench of old project detritus.**

The big move here is to get rid of the image of the perfect garage and reimagine a different result or steps along the way. If Dave keeps the picture of his old, perfect garage (*the* solution) pasted on that refrigerator door in his mind, he's never going to get anywhere, because it's too hard. Too hard doesn't work.

This isn't a gravity problem—it's not impossible. It's just that Dave's stuck because he's anchored himself to a solution that can't work.

Melanie taught sociology at a small liberal-arts college and was impressed by developments in the burgeoning fields of social innovation and social entrepreneurship that were transforming what nonprofit organizations could do using insights from the start-up and venture capital world. Knowing that students were really interested in new approaches to social impact, she started teaching a course and sponsoring social innovation projects. It went great, but she wanted to do more. She longed to make a lasting impact on her college and dreamed up a vision to found a new Institute for Social Innovation.

All she needed was fifteen million dollars to endow it properly and do it right. So she set about the task of raising the money. She developed a strategy and a killer pitch for the idea. Students loved it. Administrators were supportive. The development office hated it.

Like most small colleges, Melanie's school was underfunded and struggling to keep up. Its alumni roster was not overloaded with zillionaires, and the development office vigilantly guarded relationships with the few major donors the college had recruited. Melanie was given a long "Hands off!" list of the college's key donors, including individuals and foundations. She was free to solicit anyone not on the list, but that was it.

This was quite a setback, but Melanie had a dream worthy of her time, so she went for it. You can guess the rest. She networked and pitched tirelessly for two years—and got nowhere. She signed up a few commitments, but they were all way too small. Any big donors she discovered got scooped up by the development office for other things. Melanie's goal remained totally out of reach. Without access to the few strategic donors to the college, she'd never raise the fifteen million.

She was stuck. Unnecessarily.

Melanie believed that her problem was getting fifteen million dollars to fund her social innovation institute. But that wasn't her problem; that was just her first idea of a solution to her problem, and she got so anchored to that idea that she was mired in stuckness and failure. Oh, and did we mention that she was getting depressed by all this rejection, and that her teaching was suffering from the fund-raising distraction, and that her colleagues, sick of the Melanie money lament, had begun avoiding her? You see, when you anchor yourself to a bad solution, it just gets worse and worse with time.

Melanie's real problem was wanting to make a lasting impact on her college through social innovation—not funding an institute. She made a classic mistake of jumping to one solution too quickly. With help, Melanie got unstuck by adopting a design thinking mind-set, remembering what her real problem was, and exploring some prototypes. She realized that she'd come up with the institute idea (and its fifteen-million-dollar price tag) all on her own one day and had never really considered alternatives. She applied the mind-set of curiosity to the situation and did some more investigating before finally settling on just what it was she was trying to do.

She decided to frame an interesting question and talk to lots of people on campus. She began interviewing campus leaders, asking, "How do you think social innovation can be a part of our college, and where would we start?" She had lots of great conversations and got lots of ideas. People suggested theme dorms, alternative spring-break programming, a summer internship program, and a new senior thesis project curriculum. There were lots of ways to make an institutional impact on the college without having to start (and fund) a new institute. Sure, the institute would be cooler and bigger and sexier and would maybe even have more of an impact, but it was also nearly impossible. The other ideas were much cheaper and also enlisted more new supporters, so Melanie was no longer the sole advocate on campus. She formed a joint student-faculty team, and they concluded that a social-innovation theme dorm was the best idea.

So they prototyped it. First they canvassed all the existing theme dorms to see what they were doing that worked and didn't work. In the process, they met the students who liked the new dorm idea. The team invited those students to form a club on campus as a first step. The club ran for two years to test projects, work the idea into the campus culture, and build credibility. Then four club members jointly applied to be resident assistants in the same dorm their senior year and got the dorm manager's permission to run a social-innovation pilot program the next year. It went great, and was renewed the following year. The year after that, the dorm was officially themed for social innovation, Melanie was named its faculty adviser, and the VP of student housing became its staunch-est advocate.

By reframing the problem, using curiosity, prototyping, and a little radical collaboration, Melanie made a permanent change in the campus culture and the housing system. She had a lasting impact on the institution, without ever having to fund an institute.

John also had an anchor problem. Ever since hearing about it when he was a Boy Scout, he had dreamed of taking the mule trip from the rim to the bottom of the Grand Canyon, and promised himself that one day he would do it. Then life got in the way; he had a career to launch and a family to start. No problem—he would make the trip with his wife and kids and create an awesome family memory. But by the time John could afford that vacation for his family of five, he'd grown in size, too, and now weighed in at 221 pounds. The mule rider limit was 200 pounds. Every spring for five years, John went on a diet to try to get down to 199 pounds so he could make the trip that summer. One year he dieted down to 212, another year 208. Once he got to 203 (well . . . 209 fully dressed with a water bottle). He was getting better at dieting, but not fast enough. His kids were getting older and had other plans for their summer than hanging around donkeys with their parents for three days.

It never happened. That family memory doesn't exist.

John got anchored to his idea about the solution. It had to be the mule ride. If he'd stepped back and recognized that his one solution, though not impossible, was taking too long to achieve and had a lousy chance of success, he could have saved it. He could have reframed the idea from "Take the Grand Canyon Mule Ride" to "See the Grand Canyon Top to Bottom." There were lots of ways to do that—by helicopter, by river, and by foot. John's chances of training successfully for the hike up and down that trail were about ten times better than his chances of ever tipping the scales under 200.

The moral to the stories of Dave, Melanie, and John is this: Don't make a doable problem into an anchor problem by wedding yourself irretrievably to a solution that just isn't working. Reframe the solution to some other possibilities, prototype those ideas (take some test hikes), and get yourself unstuck. Anchor problems keep us stuck because we can only see one solution—the one we already have that doesn't work. Anchor problems are not only about our current, failed approach. They are really about the fear that, no matter what else we try, that won't work either, and then we'll have to admit that we're permanently stuck—meaning we're screwed—and we'd rather be stuck than screwed. Sometimes it is more comfortable to hold on to our familiar, failed approach to the problem than to risk a worse failure by attempting the big changes that we think will be required to eliminate it. This is a pretty common but paradoxical human behavior. Change is always uncertain, and there is no guarantee of success, no matter how hard you try. It makes sense to be fearful. The way forward is to reduce the risk (and the fear) of failure by designing a series of small prototypes to test the waters. It is okay for prototypes to fail—they are supposed to—but well-designed prototypes teach you something about the future.

Prototypes lower your anxiety, ask interesting questions, and get you data about the potential of the change that you are trying to accomplish. One of the principles of design thinking is that you want to "fail fast and fail forward," into your next step. When you're stuck with an anchor problem, try reframing the challenge as an exploration of possibilities (instead of trying to solve your huge problem in one miraculous leap), then decide to try a series of small, safe prototypes of the change you'd like to see happen. It should result in getting unstuck and finding a more creative approach to your problem. We will talk a lot more about proto-typing in chapter 6.

Before we leave the topic of anchor problems entirely, we need to make clear how they differ from the gravity problems mentioned in chapter 1. They are both really nasty problem types that keep people stuck, but they're entirely different in nature. An anchor problem is a real problem, just a hard one. It's actionable—but we've been stuck on it so long or so often that it seems insur-mountable (which is why such a problem has to be reframed, then opened up with new ideas, then knocked down to size by prototyping). Gravity problems aren't actually problems. They're circumstances that you can do nothing to change. There is no solution to a gravity problem—only acceptance and redirection. You can't defy the laws of nature, nor do we live in a world where poets reliably make a million dollars a year. Life designers know that if a problem isn't actionable, then it's not solvable. Designers may be artful at reframing and inventing, but they know better than to go up against the laws of nature or the marketplace.

We are here to get you unstuck.

We want you to have lots of ideas and lots of options.

When you have lots of ideas, you can build prototypes of your life and test them out. That's what life designers do.

Mind Mapping with Your Good Time Journal

If you didn't do your Good Time Journal in the last chapter, please go back and do it now; you are going to need it for this exercise. We are going to do three different mind maps, each one extending out at least three or four layers, and with at least a dozen or more elements in the outermost ring.

Mind Map 1—Engagement

From your Good Time Journal, pick one of the areas of greatest interest to you, or an activity during which you were really engaged (e.g., balancing the budget or pitching a new idea), and make it the center of your map. Then generate a bunch of con-nected words and concepts, using the mind-mapping technique.

Mind Map 2—Energy

From your Good Time Journal, pick something you've identified as really energizing you in your work and life (e.g., art class, giving feedback to colleagues, health-care access, keeping things running right) and mind-map this out.

Mind Map 3—Flow

From your Good Time Journal, pick one of the experiences when you were in a state of flow, put the experience itself at the center of a mind map, and complete your mapping of your experience with this state (e.g., speaking in front of a large audience or brain-storming creative ideas).

Now that you've done these three mind maps, we're going to invent an interesting, though not necessarily practical, life alterna-tive from each.

1. **Look at the outer ring of one of your maps and pick three disparate items that catch your eye. You'll know which ones they are intuitively—they should literally "jump out" at you.**
2. **Now try to combine those three items into a possible job description that would be fun and interesting to you and would be helpful to someone**

else (again, it need not be practical or appeal to lots of people or employers).

3. Name your role and draw a napkin sketch of it (a quick visual drawing of what it is), like the one shown here. For example, when Grant (who was languishing away at the car-rental agency) did this exercise based on when he was engaged in his life (hiking in redwoods, playing pickup basketball, helping his niece and nephew), he ended up drawing a sketch of himself leading a Pirate Surf Camp for children.

4. Do this exercise three times—once for each of your mind maps—making sure that the three versions are different from one another.

Now What?

You might now be thinking, "This is terrific! There are some really cool ideas here I can definitely use!" If so, that's great—but it's not guaranteed and it's not typical.

Or . . . you might have completed this and are now saying to yourself, "Well, *that* was silly! What the heck is the point of coming up with all these random nonsense ideas?" If that's you, you didn't get your money's worth out of the exercise. The whole point was to defer judgment and quiet your internal problem-finding critic. If you never did, you probably found the exercise pretty silly. If that's you, welcome to the club of smart modern people trying to do the right thing (which is to get the right answer right away). Take another look at your work, and find out if you can see it in a new light, or come back and try again in a few days.

Or you might be thinking, "Well, that was pretty fun and interesting, but I'm not really sure what I'm getting out of this yet." If that sounds like you, you're doing great. The point of this exercise isn't to generate a specific result; it's to get your mind going all over the place and ideating without judgment. By taking the exercise all the way to imagining how to combine elements creatively into surprising roles or jobs, you've successfully moved out of problem solving (what do I *do* next?) into design thinking (what can I imagine?). Now you're working with a designer's mind-set, and you've got lots of important ideas down on paper in a creative format.

It's time to start the task of innovating three real alternative lives.

It's time for your Odyssey Plans.

Try Stuff
Mind Mapping

1. Review your Good Time Journal and note activities in which you were engaged, energized, and in flow.

2. Choose an activity that you were engaged in, an activity that you felt highly energized from, and something you did that brought you into flow, and create three mind maps—one for each.

3. Look at the outer ring of each mind map, pick three things that jump out at you, and create a job description from them.

4. Create a role for each job description, and draw a napkin sketch.

5

Design Your Lives

You are legion.

Each of us is many.

This life you are living is one of many lives you will live.

Now, we are not talking about reincarnation, or anything with religious implications. The plain and simple truth is that you will live many different lives in this lifetime. If the life you are currently living feels a bit off, don't worry; life design gives you endless mulligans. You can do it over at any point, at any time. "Correction shots" are always allowed.

Working with adults of all ages, we've found that where people go wrong (regardless of their age, education, or career path) is thinking they just need to come up with a *plan* for their lives and it will be smooth sailing. If only they make the *right* choice (the *best, true, only* choice), they will have a blueprint for who they will be, what they will do, and how they will live. It's a paint-by-numbers approach to life, but in reality, life is more of an abstract painting—one that's open to multiple interpretations.

Chung was stressing out. He'd worked hard all through his career at UC Berkeley and was graduating with honors. He expected to go to graduate school eventually, but wanted to have some experience first in his chosen profession so that he could get the most out of grad school and launch his career quickly. To keep his options open, Chung applied to six different internship programs, varying from one to three years in length. Then something awful happened. He was accepted into four of the six internship programs, including his top three choices. Getting in wasn't awful; it was what happened next. Total indecision. He had no idea what to do, and no idea how to solve the age-old problem of not knowing what to do.

He was completely unprepared for getting into his three top choices, and, to exacerbate the problem, his three top choices were completely different from one another. One was teaching in rural Asia, one was doing paralegal work with an anti–sex-slavery nonprofit in Belgium, and one was doing research at a health-care think tank in Washington, D.C. They were all great, but which one to take?

Chung knew that this was an incredibly important decision, because where he did his internship would direct his graduate studies, and what he got his graduate degree in would direct his career, and that would set his life path. If he didn't *get it right,* he risked ending up in a "second choice" life. But he didn't know what his first choice was. He didn't know which was best.

Chung was making a very common mistake. He thought there was one best way to spend his life, and he had to know what it was or he'd be settling for second best—or worse. But that's not true. We all contain enough energy and talents and interests to live many different types of lives, all of which could be authentic and interesting and productive. Asking which life is best is asking a silly question; it's like asking whether it's better to have hands or feet.

After Chung came to office hours, Dave asked him, "If you're having such a hard time picking, are you sure you even have to? If you could do all three internships, one after another, how would you like that?" Chung replied, "I'd *love* to do that! But is that even allowed? How do I get permission to do all three?"

"Just ask. You've got nothing to lose by asking."

He did, and, to his great surprise, two of the organizations were willing to wait; he could do all three over the next five years if he wanted to.

It dawned on Chung, finally, that the reason he couldn't figure out which one was best was that there was no best. There were three great and totally different possibilities in front of him. At this point in his life, he could afford to check them all out, and that's what he did.

Of course, what finally happened was something Chung had never imagined at all. During his first, two-year internship, he stayed in contact with his other undergraduate buddies, talking and Skyping regularly. After about nine months, all of them except Chung found themselves unhappy and disillusioned with life after college. That wasn't so surprising. Leaving college is pretty stressful, and Chung was having some struggles on the job himself, but what was different was how everybody felt about it. Chung had learned life design. He had tools he could use, and accepted that there was more than one happy path he could chart his life by. His buddies didn't have that confidence, so Chung started spending time helping each of them figure out what they could do next. He loved doing that. In fact, he loved it so much that he decided to investigate how he could do the same kind of helping all the time. Right after that first internship, he canceled the next two and went to grad school in career counseling. After finally accepting that there were at least three great careers he could live into well, he discovered a fourth. That's the sort of thing that happens when you stop trying to "get it right" and start designing your way forward.

Dysfunctional Belief: *I need to figure out my best possible life, make a plan, and then execute it.*
Reframe: *There are multiple great lives (and plans) within me, and I get to choose which one to build my way forward to next.*

Embrace Your Multiple Personalities

One of the most powerful ways to design your *life* is to design your *lives.* No, we haven't hit our heads and that isn't a typo. We're going to ask you to imagine and write up three different versions of the next five years of your life. We call these Odyssey Plans. Whether or not three interesting variations of your next five years immediately leap onto the screens in the multiplex movie theater in your head or not, we know you've got at least three viable and substantially different possibilities in you. We all do. Every single one of the thousands of people we've worked with has proved us correct in this. We all have lots of lives within us. We certainly have three at any particular moment. Of course, we can only live out one at a time, but we want to ideate multiple variations in order to choose creatively and generatively.

Now, it may seem a daunting task to come up with three different plans, but you can do it. Everyone we've worked with has done it, and so can you. You may well have a preferred plan already in mind. That's fine. You may even have a plan that you've committed to and that is well under way. That's fine, too—you still need to develop three Odyssey Plan alternatives. Really. Some of the people who've gotten the most out of this exercise are the ones who entered into it already having all the answers to their One True Plan in place. The value of conceiving multiple prototypes in parallel (like these three Odyssey Plans) has been validated by research at the Stanford Graduate School of Education. A team led by Professor Dan Schwartz evaluated two groups.[1] One started with three ideas in parallel, then subsequently had two more ideas on the way to their final idea. The second team started with one idea and then iterated four more times. Each team generated five rounds of ideas, but the parallel team did much better— generating more ideas and clearly better final solutions. The serial team—who started with just one idea—tended to keep refining the same idea over and over, never really innovating. The conclusion is that if your mind starts with multiple ideas in parallel, it is not prematurely committed to one path and stays more open and able to receive and conceive more novel innovations. Designers have known this all along—you don't want to start with just one idea, or you're likely to get stuck with it.

Try not to think of your Odyssey Plans as "Plan A, Plan B, and Plan C"—where A is the really good plan and B is the okay plan and C is the plan that you really hope you don't get stuck with but that you would accept as tolerable if absolutely necessary. Every Odyssey Plan is a Plan A, because it's really you and it's really possible. Odyssey Plans are sketches of possibilities that can animate your imagination and help you choose which wayfinding direction you will actually take to start prototyping and living into next.

Don't worry about choosing which alternative life you are going to live. We have great ideas and tools for the difficult task of "choosing," and we'll discuss them in chapter 9. Criteria for choosing what's next may be based on available resources (proximity, time, money), coherence (how the alternative fits into your Lifeview and Workview), your confidence level (do you believe you can do this?), and how much you like it. But first things first. You need to develop the alternatives.

So Many Lives, So Little Time

We call these Odyssey Plans because life is an odyssey—an adventurous journey into the future with hopes and goals, helpers, lovers and antagonists, unknowns and serendipities, all unfolding over time in a way we both intend at the start and weave together as we go. Homer[2] told the ancient story of Odysseus as a metaphor for this life-as-adventure. So we want to take the time now to imagine multiple ways you could launch the next chapter of your life's journey—your quest.

We want you to create three very different plans for the next five years of your life. Why five years? Because two years is too short (makes us nervous that we haven't thought far enough ahead) and seven years is too long (we know stuff is going to happen to change things by then). In fact, if you listen to people tell their stories, most people's lives are actually lived as a series of two-to-four-year seasons strung together. Even important longer periods (the child-rearing years) are broken into substantially distinct two-to-four-year chunks—the toddler years, the preschool years, the tween years, the years when they don't speak to you, also called the teen years. Five years cover one good four-year chunk with an extra year of buffer time. After doing this exercise many different ways and thousands of times with people of all ages, we're confident five years is about right. Just try it.

We want to insist (since we won't be grading your homework) that you create three very different alternative versions of you. Three plans give you real choices (a list of three feels much longer than a list of two), and will stretch your creative muscles hard enough that you'll know you didn't just opt for the obvious answer. We want you to come up with three truly different alternatives—not three variations on a theme. Living in a commune in Vermont and living in a kibbutz in Israel aren't really two alternatives; they're two versions of the same alternative. Try to come up with three really different ideas.

We know you can do this because we've seen thousands of people do it successfully, including lots of people who started out convinced they couldn't possibly come up with three alternative ideas about what life they might live. If you're one of those people, here's a way to quickly come up with "three versions of my life."

Life One—That Thing You Do. Your first plan is centered on what you've already got in mind—either your current life expanded forward or that hot idea you've been nursing for some time. This is the idea you already have—it's a good one and it deserves attention in this exercise.

Life Two—That Thing You'd Do If Thing One Were Suddenly Gone. It happens. Some kinds of work come to an end. Almost no one makes buggy whips or Internet browsers anymore. The former are out of date and the latter are given away free with your operating system, so buggy whips and browsers don't make for hot careers. Just imagine that your life one idea is suddenly over or no longer an option. What would you do? You can't not make a living. You can't do nothing. What would you do? If you're like most people we talk with, when you really force your imagination to believe that you *have* to make a living doing something other than doing That Thing You Do, you'll come up with something.

Life Three—The Thing You'd Do or the Life You'd Live If Money or Image Were No Object. If you knew you could make a decent living at it and you knew no one would laugh at you or think less of you for doing it—what would you do? We're not saying you suddenly can make a living doing this and we can't promise no one will laugh (though they rarely do), but we are saying imagining this alternative can be a very useful part of your life design exploration.

Dave was speaking to a young MBA student recently who was convinced that he didn't have three ideas about his life.

"So what are you going to do?" Dave asked the young MBA.

"I want to go into management consulting."

"Great, that's your life one," Dave replied. "But guess what? All the CEOs in the world just got together and concluded that they really hadn't been all that helped by all those billions of dollars spent on consulting, so they all decided to stop buying any more. Consulting just died. What'll you do now?"

The MBA was shocked. "What! No consulting at all?!"

"Nope—none. You gotta do something else. What's it gonna be?"

"Well, if I couldn't do consulting, I guess I'd try to work inside a big media company working on strategy or marketing communications."

"Great! That's your life two!"

When asked what he'd do if money or image were no object, and after being reassured that no one would laugh or make fun of him, the young man proposed his life three.

"Well, I'd really like to go into wine distribution. It always seemed a little silly, but frankly it fascinates me and I'd love to try it."

"Okay," said Dave, "there are your three lives."

We've run through a similar dialogue with people who were stuck on only one idea for their lives. If you can't come up with three ideas quickly, just try this approach to your life one, life two, and life three, and you'll probably find yourself getting more than enough ideas.

Don't get stuck. Don't overthink it. But do really do it.

It's an exercise that will change your life.

Literally.

Odyssey Planning 101

Create three alternative versions of the next five years of your life. Each one must include:

1. A visual/graphical timeline. Include personal and noncareer events as well—do you want to be married, train to win the CrossFit Games, or learn how to bend spoons with your mind?
2. A title for each option in the form of a six-word headline describing the essence of this alternative.
3. Questions that this alternative is asking—preferably two or three. A good designer asks questions to test assumptions and reveal new insights. In each potential timeline, you will investigate different possibilities and learn different things about yourself and the world. What kinds of things will you want to test and explore in each alternative version of your life?
4. A dashboard where you can gauge
   a. Resources (Do you have the objective resources—time, money, skill, contacts—you need to pull off your plan?)
   b. Likability (Are you hot or cold or warm about your plan?)
   c. Confidence (Are you feeling full of confidence, or pretty uncertain about pulling this off?)
   d. Coherence (Does the plan make sense within

itself? And is it consistent with you, your
Workview, and your Lifeview?)

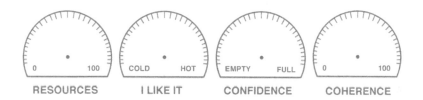

RESOURCES   I LIKE IT   CONFIDENCE   COHERENCE

- **Possible considerations**

  - **Geography—where will you live?**
  - **What experience/learning will you gain?**
  - **What are the impacts/results of choosing this alternative?**
  - **What will life look like? What particular role, industry, or company do you see yourself in?**

- **Other ideas**

  - **Do keep in mind things other than career and money. Even though those things are important, if not central, to the decisive direction of your next few years, there are other critical elements that you want to pay attention to.**
  - **Any of the considerations listed above can be a springboard for forming your alternative lives for the next five years. If you find yourself stuck, try making a mind map out of any of the design considerations listed above. Don't overthink this exercise, and don't skip it.**

For all of us, Odyssey Plans can define important things still to do in our lives, and help us remember dreams we may have forgotten. That twelve-year-old astronaut you once were is still there. Be curious about what else you might discover. Try making at least one of these plans at least a little bit wild. Even if it's something you would never do in your right mind, write down your most far-fetched and crazy idea. Maybe it's giving up all your worldly possessions and living off the grid in Alaska or India. Maybe it's taking acting classes and trying to make it in Hollywood. Perhaps it's becoming an expert skateboarder or devoting your life to adrenaline-producing extreme sports. Or maybe it's hunting down that long-lost great-uncle and filling in the gaps of your family story. You may want to do different alternative plans for different areas of your life: alternatives for career, for love, for health, or for play. Or you may want to combine these elements. The only wrong way to do this is to not do it at all.

Martha's Many Lives

What follows is an example of three five-year Odyssey Plans from a participant in one of our Mid-Career Workshops. Martha is a technology executive who was looking to try something more meaningful for the latter half of her life. She came up with three very different plans for her future, each a little more risky and innovative, but all involving some kind of community building.

Her three plans were: doing her first Silicon Valley–style start-up, becoming the CEO of a nonprofit working with at-risk kids, and opening a fun and friendly neighborhood bar in the Haight-Ashbury district of San Francisco, where she lived. Note that each example has a six-word headline describing the plan, a four-gauge dashboard (we really like dashboards), and the three questions that this particular alternative plan is asking.

Example 1

Title: "All In—The Silicon Valley Story"

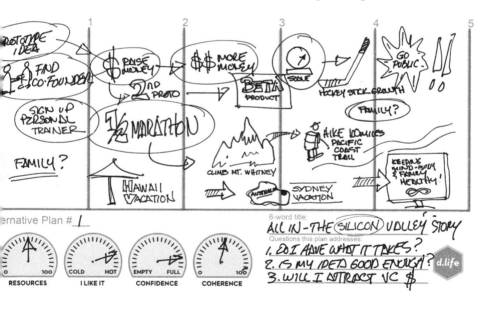

Questions

1. "Do I have what it takes to be an entrepreneur?"
2. "Is my idea good enough?"
3. "Will I be able to raise venture capital money?"

Example 2

Title: "Using What I Know—Helping Kids!"

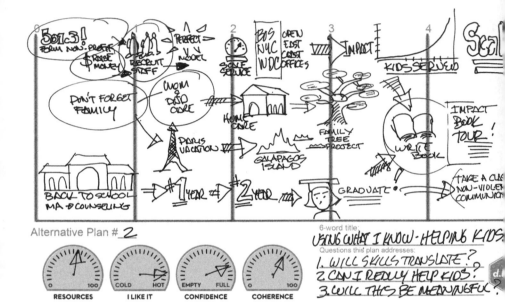

Alternative Plan #_2_

RESOURCES · **I LIKE IT** · **CONFIDENCE** · **COHERENCE**

6-word title: USING WHAT I KNOW - HELPING KIDS

Questions this plan addresses:
1. WILL SKILLS TRANSLATE?
2. CAN I REALLY HELP KIDS?
3. WILL THIS BE MEANINGFUL?

Questions

1. "Will my skills translate to the nonprofit world?"
2. "Can I really help at-risk kids with a nonprofit?"
3. "Will this be meaningful?"

Example 3

Title: "Creating Community—One Drink at a Time!"

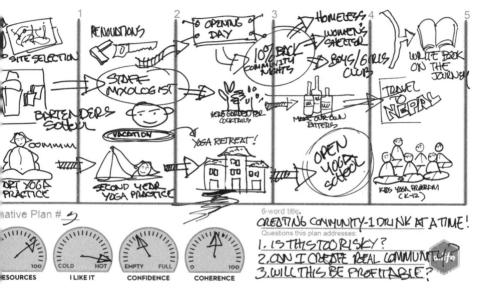

Questions:

1. "Am I ready to take this much risk?"
2. "Can I really create true community with a bar?"
3. "Will this be profitable?"

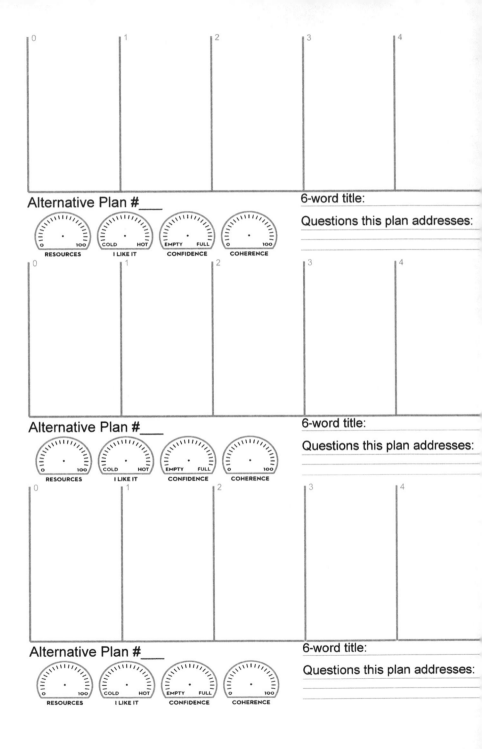

| 0 | 1 | 2 | 3 | 4 |

Alternative Plan #____

RESOURCES I LIKE IT CONFIDENCE COHERENCE

6-word title:

Questions this plan addresses:

| 0 | 1 | 2 | 3 | 4 |

Alternative Plan #____

RESOURCES I LIKE IT CONFIDENCE COHERENCE

6-word title:

Questions this plan addresses:

| 0 | 1 | 2 | 3 | 4 |

Alternative Plan #____

RESOURCES I LIKE IT CONFIDENCE COHERENCE

6-word title:

Questions this plan addresses:

Odyssey Plan Exercise

Now complete three alternative five-year plans of your own, one on each of the three worksheets here or downloadable at www .designingyour.life.

Sharing the Three Versions of You

We're going to ask you to share your Odyssey Plan alternatives. Don't freak out. There is huge magic in having three versions of you. Mostly, it helps you realize that there isn't a single right answer to what's next for you. Consider which alternative rates high on resources, likability, confidence, and coherence. Which version of you gives you that jazzy, feel-good, light-my-fire kind of feeling? Which version feels draining?

The best way to interact with your alternatives is to share them aloud with a group of friends—ideally, with your Life Design Team (see chapter 11 for more on team and community) or the group you are reading this book with, as we suggested in the introduction. The most fun and effective way to go through the life design process is to do it in a group of three to six people, including yourself, who meet as a team. It can work fine if the only person doing life design is you, but a group is highly preferable, with everyone both doing the work and supporting the others' life designs. It may be easier than you think to find two to five other people willing to do this with you. Just give the book away to a few likely suspects, get together to discuss it, and see what you find. You may be surprised. And we're not just trying to get you to buy more books (though our publisher would be pleased if you did!)—it's just an easy way to start the conversation.

In any event, whether you form a Life Design Team that meets regularly or not, you'll want to present your Odyssey Plans to a group of supporters to get feedback and ideas. You want to invite people who will ask good questions but not offer critiques or unwanted advice. The ground rules for listening are these: Tell your listeners not to critique, review, or advise. You want them to receive, reflect, and amplify. Find two to five people who are "there for you" and will show up for an evening dedicated to helping you design your life (or who are willing to read this chapter, at the very least). When it's time for questions, "Tell me more about . . ." is a great approach that keeps the inquiry supportive. If you really don't want to or can't find a group to share with, then video yourself presenting your Odyssey Plans and watch and listen to yourself as though you weren't the author; then see what you have to say to yourself and jot down your ideas.

Life design is about generating options, and this exercise of designing multiple lives will guide you in whatever's next for you. You aren't designing the rest of your life; you are designing what's next. Every possible version of you holds unknowns and compromises, each with its own identifiable and unintended consequences. You are not so much finding answers in this exercise as learning to embrace and explore the questions, and be curious about the possibilities.

Remember, there are multiple great lives within you.

You are legion.

And you get to choose which prototype to start working on next.

Try Stuff
Odyssey Plan

1. **Create three alternative five-year plans, using the worksheet provided.**

2. **Give each alternative a descriptive six-word title, and write down three questions that arise out of each version of you.**

3. **Complete each gauge on the dashboard— ranking each alternative for resources, likability, confidence, and coherence.**

4. **Present your plan to another person, a group, or your Life Design Team. Note how each alternative energizes you.**

6

Prototyping

Clara needed to redesign her life. After thirty-five years of building a successful career as a sales executive in the hi-tech world, she was done. All Clara knew was that she wanted a life that didn't involve meeting a sales quota every quarter. In fact, she didn't even want to hear the words "sales quota" ever again. Many of her friends had spent the last two decades developing side interests—hobbies they were turning into professions, creative interests they were now pursuing full-time, and volunteer work that gave them meaning and purpose. All her friends seemed to be leaving their professional careers to pursue something else—but Clara didn't have a "something else." She had spent most of her life raising children as a single mom and developing her career in sales. Her children were adults now, her career was coming to a close, and Clara had no idea where to begin, or what might be next, so we helped her start from right where she was and design her way forward.

Clara's friends had lots of suggestions for her, and most of them agreed that the important thing was to "Just get going! If you don't have a good idea, then just pick something and jump in. You're too young to quit now. Whatever you do, don't get stuck bored at home—just *commit to something.*" That was easy advice for them to give, since all of them at least knew how they wanted to invest their time. Clara didn't. So where to begin? Clara made a great decision. She recognized that it was good advice to "do something," but it was bad advice to "jump in and just commit to something" because she could easily find herself overcommitted to the wrong thing. What she needed to do was find a way of trying things out first without committing herself to them prematurely. She wanted to test-drive some possibilities, get some real experience, but do it in water up to her knees, not over her head.

Even though she didn't have a specific goal in mind for what she'd later call her encore career, Clara did have one possible area of interest. She'd been one of the first women ever to sell mainframe computers for IBM and had long considered herself a feminist. She figured, "Okay, that's still an issue worth working on—let's look for something to do with helping women." From that moment on, she was actively researching approaches to helping women and keeping her eye out for things she could try. A few weeks later, she was at her local church when a woman was giving a talk about mediation and nonviolent communication and how these techniques were being used to help mothers with delinquent children and battered women in abusive marriages. Clara introduced herself to the woman and started asking questions about her work. These sharp questions got her invited to attend the training class on mediation. It was only a few hours a week, and even if she passed the certification test at the end, there was no obligation, so she did it to get some experience of what it was like to do mediation for troubled women. She took the course and got a mediation certificate.

It turned out that there was an opening for a very difficult job, providing mediation services for youth in the juvenile justice system. The position was funded only through the calendar year, so they couldn't promise how long it would last, but that was fine for Clara. She would be mediating among the courts, the schools, the parents, and the kids, and coming up with an alternative to incarceration for at-risk children. It was a hard place to start, but Clara found that her decades of dealing with difficult salespeople in the hi-tech world made her a natural negotiator and problem solver. Also, many of the juvenile offenders had single moms, and she had a special place in her heart for other struggling single mothers. Clara found the offer surprisingly attractive. She was ready to try it—though just part-time, and just until the end of the year. She was still exploring.

Clara continued searching for ways to get involved in women's issues, and discovered the Women's Foundation of California (WFC). WFC didn't do anything on its own—it funded other nonprofits that were geared toward a wide range of social justice issues related to women. It was a vantage point for her "try stuff out" exploration project, so she reached out to the organization. Clara's mediation work impressed the WFC leadership, and she was invited to join. During the course of the three years she spent serving this foundation, she learned about grant writing and nonprofit funding, and she also learned a great deal about twenty-seven different nonprofits that were hard at work solving social problems in her region.

Along the way, Clara found that she was not drawn to staying involved in the legal system as a mediator (as important as that work was), but she was increasingly drawn to the issue of homelessness, which hits women especially hard. Through WFC, she met a philanthropist who was the largest benefactor for the homeless shelter in her hometown. He asked Clara to become a member of the shelter's board of directors, and it was at that moment that she realized she'd found her encore career. She took his offer and dropped everything else. She is now a champion for the homeless in her city, and is pioneering a model to solve homelessness locally and nationally.

Clara didn't start out with a plan to work for the homeless. Knowing that she hadn't found a specific mission to direct her steps, she carefully and thoughtfully crafted a series of small but illustrative experiences and involvements to design her way forward. Her path to "homeless champion" (which, by the way, has become her passion) was not a straight line, by any means. She designed the life she is living, step by step, by thinking like a designer and building her way forward by doing small experiments—prototypes. She trusted that if she kept giving herself carefully selected hands-on encounters, she'd find her way.

She took a class on mediation. She took the job in the juvenile justice system. She joined the women's foundation. She learned about the world of nonprofits. She got involved in the board for the homeless center. By doing the work, meeting the people, and choosing to explore her options through hands-on experience, and not just spending her time reading, thinking, or reflecting in her journal about what she should or could do next, Clara found her encore career. It was only through life design that she was able to discover a future that had been not only unknowable, but also unimaginable. Clara did it, and you can, too.

Dysfunctional Belief: *If I comprehensively research the best data for all aspects of my plan, I'll be fine.*
Reframe: *I should build prototypes to explore questions about my alternatives.*

Prototyping—Why and How

"Building is thinking" is a phrase you will often hear around the Design Program at Stanford. When that idea is coupled with the bias-to-action mind-set, you get a lot of building and thinking. If you ask people what they are doing, they will tell you that they are building prototypes. They might be prototyping new product ideas, new consumer experiences, or new services. At Stanford, we believe anything can be prototyped, from a physical object to public policy. Prototyping is such an integral part of design thinking that it might be worthwhile to step back a little and make sure that the "why" of prototyping is as well understood as the "how."

When you are trying to solve a problem, any problem, you typically start with what you know about the problem: you start with the data. You need enough data so that you can understand what causes what, and what is likely to happen when something else happens.

Unfortunately, when you are designing your life, you don't have a lot of data available, especially reliable data about your future. You have to accept that this is the kind of messy problem in which traditional cause-and-effect thinking won't work. Luckily, designers have come up with a way of sneaking up on the future through prototyping.

When we use the term "prototyping" in design thinking, we do not mean making something to check whether your solution is right. We don't mean creating a representation of a completed design, nor do we mean making just one thing (designers make *lots of prototypes*—never just *a prototype*). Prototyping the life design way is all about asking good questions, outing our hidden biases and assumptions, iterating rapidly, and creating momentum for a path we'd like to try out.

Prototypes should be designed to ask a question and get some data about something that you're interested in. Good prototypes isolate one aspect of a problem and design an experience that allows you to "try out" some version of a potentially interesting future. Prototypes help you visualize alternatives in a very experiential way. That allows you to imagine your future as if you are already living it. Creating new experiences through prototyping will give you an opportunity to understand what a new career path might feel like, even if only for an hour or a day. And prototyping helps you involve others early and helps build a community of folks who are interested in your journey and your life design. Prototypes are a great way to start a conversation, and, more often than not, one thing typically leads to another. Prototypes frequently turn into unexpected opportunities—they help serendipity happen. Finally, prototypes allow you to try and fail rapidly without overinvesting in a path before you have any data.

Our philosophy is that it is always possible to prototype something you are interested in. The best way to get started is to keep your first few prototypes very low-resolution and very simple. You want to isolate one variable and design a prototype to answer that one question. Use what you have available or can ask for, and be prepared to iterate quickly. And remember that a prototype is not a thought experiment; it must involve a physical experience in the world. The data to make good decisions are found in the real world, and prototyping is the best way to engage that world and get the data you need to move forward.

Prototyping is also about building empathy and understanding. Our prototyping process inevitably requires collaboration, working with others. Everyone is on a journey, and your prototype encounters with others will reveal their life designs and give you ideas for your own life.

So—we prototype to ask good questions, create experiences, reveal our assumptions, fail fast, fail forward, sneak up on the future, and build empathy for ourselves and others. Once you accept that this is really the only way to get the data you need, prototyping becomes an integral part of your life design process. Not only is it true that doing prototyping is a good idea; it's equally true that not prototyping is a bad and sometimes very costly idea.

Slow and Steady

Elise didn't need to prototype—she was ready to *go*. After spending years working in human resource departments in large corporations, Elise was ready for a change. A big change. Now. She loved food, especially Italian food, and she loved the experiences she'd had in small cafés and deli markets in Tuscany. It was her dream to run a great Italian deli with a small café inside that served wonderful coffee and authentic Tuscan food. She decided to go for it. She had saved enough to get started, collected all the recipes she needed, researched the best place near her home to locate such a business, and did it. She rented a place, totally renovated it, stocked it with the best products, and opened to great fanfare. It was an immense amount of work, and it was a roaring success. Everyone loved it. She was busier than ever. And in no time she was miserable.

She hadn't prototyped her idea at all. She didn't sneak up on her future. She jumped out of the plane right into it. She hadn't tried out what it was like working in a café, day in and day out. She hadn't discovered that she had assumed that running a café was the same as going to a café or planning a café. She learned the hard way that she's a great café designer and renovation project manager, and a lousy deli manager. She didn't enjoy hiring staff (over and over), or tracking inventory, or ordering new stock, and don't even ask about the maintenance. She was stuck with this successful store and didn't know what to do. Eventually, she sold it and went into restaurant interior design, but she got there by a very painful path.

How could she have prototyped her idea? She could have tried catering first—an easy business to start up and shut down (no rent, few employees, super-portable, no regular hours). She could have gotten a job bussing tables at an Italian deli to have a good look at the dirty end of the job, not just the sexy menu planning. She could have interviewed three happy and three grumpy deli-café owners to learn which group she was more like. We met Elise after it was all over. We heard her story when she was taking a

Life Design Workshop with us. After the workshop she lamented, "Gosh, if only I'd taken the slow path of prototyping first, I'd have saved myself so much time!" So, yes, even if you're in a rush, we recommend you prototype your life ideas. You'll get a better design and save a lot of time and difficulty.

Prototype Conversations— Life Design Interview

Once you've committed yourself to life design prototyping, how do you do it? The simplest and easiest form of prototyping is a conversation. We're going to describe a specific form of prototype conversation that we call a Life Design Interview.

A Life Design Interview is incredibly simple. It just means getting someone's story. Not just anyone and not just any story, of course. You want to talk to someone who is either doing and living what you're contemplating, or has real experience and expertise in an area about which you have questions. And the story you're after is the personal story of how that person got to be doing that thing he or she does, or got the expertise he has and what it's really like to do what she does.

You want to hear what the person who does what you might someday want to do loves and hates about his job. You want to know what her days look like, and then you want to see if you can imagine yourself doing that job—and loving it—for months and years on end. In addition to asking people about their work and life, you will also be able to find out how they got there—

their career path. Most people fail not for lack of talent but for lack of imagination. You can get a lot of this information by sitting down with someone and getting his or her story. That's Life Design Interviewing. Clara had lots of these conversations, and they really helped her. Elise had almost none, and it really cost her.

The first thing to know about a Life Design Interview is what it's not—a job interview. If you find yourself in the middle of a Life Design Interview and you're answering questions or talking about yourself rather than getting the story of the person you're with, stop and flip it around. This is critical. If the person you're in conversation with misperceives that your meeting is a job interview, then it's a disaster, and your Life Design Interview has failed or will fail. It's all about mind-sets. Think about it: When someone thinks you're looking for a job, the first thing on his or her mind actually has nothing to do with you at all. He is thinking, "Do we have a job opening to discuss?" The answer to that is usually no. So most of the time you're trying to get a meeting and the other person thinks you're looking for a job, you don't get the appointment. You just get "No." It may seem like a harsh and presumptuous rejection, but it's actually the kindest and most supportive thing that person can do. If in fact you are looking for a job and that person hasn't got one to give or isn't influential in the hiring process, the best thing she can do for you is tell you so and free you to go find someone with an opening who can actually be helpful to you. It doesn't feel like an act of kindness (and most people deliver a rejection poorly), but that is what's actually happening.

If it turns out the answer to that first question is "Yes, we do have an opening available," then the second question is "Does she fit here?" The mind-set of a job interview is critique and judgment, and *that* is not the mind-set we're looking for if we are after an interesting story and a personal connection.

In fact, a Life Design Interview isn't an "interview" at all—it's really just a conversation. So, when trying to get a meeting with someone, you don't use the term "interview," because that person will assume you mean a job interview (unless you're a journalist, and that will make him even more nervous, for other reasons). All you're doing here is identifying people who are currently doing things that you're interested in and whose stories you want to get. This is way easier than you think. As soon as you've determined that Anna is a cool person doing really interesting work, you and Anna have something in common—you both think that she and what she's doing are two of your favorite topics! The essence of the request for a meeting to have this conversation is: "Hello, Anna, I'm so glad to connect with you. John said you were just the person I needed to speak with. I'm very impressed with what I know of your work, and I'd love to hear some of your story. Might you have thirty minutes to spare, at a time and place convenient to you, when I can buy you a cup of coffee and hear more about your experience?" That's about it—really. (And, yes, it's important to mention Anna's respected friend or colleague John if at all possible. John is the guy whose *referral* made all the difference in your finding Anna, and in her being more inclined to accept your request for coffee. There are lots of Annas in the world who will have coffee with you even if you weren't referred by John, but it works a lot better if you can get that referral. We'll talk about how to get referrals in chapter 8. It's called networking. Yes, you have to network to do life design effectively, but more on that later.)

Prototype Experiences

Prototype conversations are great; they're incredibly informative and easy to come by. But you're going to want more than just stories as input for coming up with your life design. You want actually to experience what "it" is really like—by watching others do it or, better yet, doing some form of it yourself. Prototype experiences allow us to learn through a direct encounter with a possible future version of us. This experiential version could involve spending a day shadowing a professional you'd like to be (Take a Friend to Work Day), or a one-week unpaid exploratory project that you create, or a three-month internship (obviously, a three-month internship requires more investment and a larger commitment). If you've conducted a good number of prototype conversations using Life Design Interviewing, then you will have met people along the way who you may be interested in observing or shadowing. So that variety of prototype should be pretty accessible for you. You just have to ask—and remember, people enjoy being helpful. Most people we work with are surprised how well their Life Design Interviews go. The people they meet with really seem to enjoy it. Asking to shadow someone at work is a much bigger favor than a thirty-minute cup of coffee, but after a dozen or so prototype conversations, you'll be ready to make a bigger request. Try it—even if you have to try a few times. You'll learn a great deal.

Coming up with hands-on prototype experiences, in which you actually get to *do stuff* and not just hear about stuff or watch stuff, is an even bigger challenge. But it's well worth the effort to get your hands dirty and really discover how something fits you.

You wouldn't buy a car without a test drive, would you? But we do this all the time with jobs and life changes. It's crazy, when you think about it. Remember all the ideas we had that Elise could have tried before she actually bought and opened a deli—things like catering a few times or taking a short-term job bussing tables? Those are the sorts of ideas you're looking for. Conceiving prototype experiences like this is real design work and is going to require having lots of ideas. So this is a great time to introduce *design brainstorming*—a collaborative technique for finding lots of ideas. Here we go.

Brainstorming Prototype Experiences

Look back at the Odyssey Plans you made in the previous chapter. We hope these sparked some future versions of you that you'd like to explore, and that you now have questions that need answers. What's it like working in a small company after all these years at Huge, Inc.? How is managing an organic farm full-time different from spending a summer WOOFing (working on an organic farm as a volunteer)? What do salespeople actually do all day, anyway? Take a closer look at whatever version of your Odyssey Plans was coherent, likable, and exciting, and that you're somewhat confident you could do. What are your questions? What would you like to understand better by prototyping the experience?

This is the challenge we're going to address by brainstorming some prototypable ideas.

Just about everyone has done something called "brainstorming" before. This is one of those often used and much-abused words that can be used to describe anything from a structured creativity exercise to just sitting in a room and tossing around ideas. Brainstorming, a technique for generating lots of creative and out-of-the-box ideas, was first described by Alex Osborn in a book published in 1953 called *Applied Imagination*. He described a method of generating ideas that relied on two rules: generating a large quantity of ideas without concern for quality, and deferring judgment so that participants would not censor ideas. Since this early description, brainstorming has become a popular way of generating ideas and innovations and has taken on many forms, but all still obey Osborn's two rules.

The most common form is group brainstorming. A group of individuals, typically four to six, get together, select a focal question or problem on which to brainstorm, and then spend a period of twenty minutes to an hour generating as many ideas as possible to solve the problem posed in the focal question. The goal is to come up with ideas that can be prototyped and tried in the real world.

Brainstorming requires a group of people who want to be helpful and who have some practice with the technique. It isn't easy to find good brainstormers, but once you have a good group, you can make a lot of progress generating life design ideas that you want to prototype. Like great improvisational jazz musicians, good brainstormers learn to focus on a topic, but they can also let go, be in-the-moment, and improvise, coming up with ideas that are truly original. It takes practice and attention, but once you master life design brainstorming, you'll never run out of ideas again.

Life design brainstorming has four steps, and a very structured approach to coming up with lots of prototypable ideas. Typically, if you are the facilitator who brings the group together, you might have already framed the brainstorming topic. You want a team of no fewer than three and rarely more than six people who have all volunteered to help. Once the group is convened, the session proceeds as follows.

1. Framing a Good Question

It is important to frame a good question for a brainstorming session. The facilitator uses the process of coming up with the question as a way to create a focus for the group's energy. When coming up with the question, the facilitator needs to be aware of some guidelines.

If the question isn't open-ended, you won't get very interesting results and not much volume. We tend to start all of our life design brainstorms with the phrase "How many ways can we think of to . . ." to make sure that we haven't limited our potential output. Clara could have organized her brainstorm around the question "How many ways can we think of to experience making an impact on women's empowerment?" Before jumping into grad school, Chung could have set up a brainstorm session asking, "What are the functions of career counseling, and what encounters can we imagine to reveal what doing each of them is really like?"

You also want to be careful not to include your solution accidentally in your question. This happens all the time with some of Bill's clients. They want to brainstorm "ten new ways to make a ladder for a stockroom." This isn't a very good framing question, because a ladder is a solution (and they only want ten ideas). A better framing would be to focus on what a ladder does: "How many ways can we think of to . . . give a person access to inventory in high places?" or "How many ways can we think of to . . . give a stockperson three-dimensional mobility in a warehouse?" These questions do not assume that ladders are the only way to solve the problem, and they open up the solution space for more creative answers (user-controlled stockroom drones, anyone?).

Also, be careful that you don't frame a question so broadly that it is meaningless. We sometimes sit in on life design brainstorms where the question is "How many ways can we think of to . . . make Bob happy?" This vague question fails for a couple of reasons: First of all, "happiness" means too many different things to different people. And positive psychology tells us that happiness is context-dependent, so, without a context—such as "my work" or "my social life"—no one knows where to start. Without some constraints, these types of brainstorming sessions tend to generate ideas that are neither prototypable nor satisfying.

Most of the time when people tell us "our brainstorm didn't work," we find out that they framed a poor question—either one that already assumed a solution or one that was so vague they couldn't get any traction for generating ideas. Watch out for this when you start to brainstorm with our four-step method.

2.   Warming Up

People need a transition from their hectic, event-driven workday to a state of relaxed, creative attention if they are going to do a good job brainstorming. People need some support and a transitional activity to move from their analytical/critical brain to a synthesizing/nonjudgmental brain. It's a mind-body problem and it takes some practice to get good at making such a transition. A good facilitator takes the lead and makes sure everyone is warmed up and feeling creative. This is essential if the brainstorm is going to be high-energy and generate a lot of ideas.

You can visit our website, www.designingyour.life, for a list of exercises and improvisational games that we use all the time with our students. Here's one quick idea that always works: give everyone in your brainstorming group a can of Play-Doh. Bill's been in love with Play-Doh since his days at the toy company Kenner Products; it is a magic material that turns adults into children again. If you just let your brainstormers play with the Play-Doh while they are brainstorming, we guarantee you will get more and better ideas.

3.   The Brainstorm Itself

As we mentioned at the start, brainstorming sessions need to be facilitated. The facilitator sets up the room and makes sure there are pens and sticky notes or paper for every participant, and that the space is quiet and comfortable. The facilitator also helps frame the question, manages the warm-up, makes sure everything that is said is recorded, and manages the rules.

We recommend that all participants have their own pens and notepads and write down their ideas. That way, the group isn't constrained by how fast the facilitator can record ideas, and there is less chance of losing a potentially great idea.

The Rules of Brainstorming

1. **Go for quantity, not quality.**
2. **Defer judgment and do not censor ideas.**
3. **Build off the ideas of others.**
4. **Encourage wild ideas.**

The "Go for quantity, not quality" rule helps set a common goal for the group, and it encourages a lot of positive energy. A good brainstorming team is bubbling with ideas, and there is rarely a pause in the output.

We use the "Defer judgment and do not censor ideas" rule to make sure that the brainstorming session is a safe place to have any crazy idea that comes to mind. People fear being judged as silly, and fear shuts down creativity. This rule helps make sure that doesn't happen.

We "Build off the ideas of others" in the same way a soloist in a jazz quartet riffs off the musical ideas of the soloist before him. We want to use the collective creativity of the group, and this rule encourages that creative interaction.

We "Encourage wild ideas" not because the wild ideas themselves are useful (they are rarely used in the final sort), but because we need to break out of the box of typical thinking. When you go far out of the box and spend some time in Crazy Land, the ideas that follow tend to be more innovative and original. Wild ideas often contain the seeds of the most useful things to prototype.

4. Naming and Framing the Outcomes

This is perhaps the most important part of a brainstorm, and the one activity that we notice most groups leave out. They might take a cell-phone picture of their wall full of sticky notes, high-five all around, and then leave. The problem with this is that the information on the wall is pretty fragile, and if it isn't processed right away, the freshness of the ideas and their interconnections get lost. Later, participants often feel that nothing happened, and they can't remember what the brainstorm accomplished.

Ideas should be counted—you want to be able to say, "We had 141 ideas." Group similar ideas together by subject or category, name those categories, and frame the results with reference to the original focal question. Every unique category is given a descriptive and often funny name that captures the essence of that group of ideas. Then vote. Voting is important, and should be done silently, so that people aren't influencing one another. We like to use colored dots to cast votes, and we also like to use categories such as:

- **Most exciting**
- **The one we wish we could do if money were no object**
- **The dark horse—probably won't work, but if it did . . .**
- **Most likely to lead to a great life**
- **If we could ignore the laws of physics . . .**

Once the voting is complete, the selections are discussed, and potentially regrouped and framed again; then decisions are made on what to prototype first.

At the end of our four-step process, the goal is to say something like "We had 141 ideas, we grouped those into six categories, and, based on our focal question, we selected eight killer ideas to prototype; then we prioritized the list, and our first prototype is . . ." Often it is possible to back off from one of the wild ideas just a little and turn it into a great idea. Let's say that Clara's brainstorm had the crazy idea of "Meet with a hundred experienced donors to women-oriented nonprofits." Clara may have felt that a hundred meetings were more than she was able to pull off, but the idea of gaining access to a large body of experience and wisdom was attractive—and prompted the derivative idea of looking for a donor group, which is exactly what she found in the Women's Foundation of California.

If you follow all four steps and get results like that, your life design brainstorming will be more than worth it. The brainstorm will generate energy and momentum toward your goal of coming up with some prototype experiences to explore. It will also be an exercise you can turn to whenever you need some new ideas, some community support, or just a little more fun in your life with people you trust.

A great way to do this would be to combine your Odyssey Plan presentation gathering (discussed in chapter 5) with a prototype experience brainstorm session. Your collaborators will have a much better time if they are able not only to give you feedback but also to contribute directly to your life design with ideas and actionable prototype possibilities.

Try Stuff
Prototyping

1. Review your three Odyssey Plans and the questions you wrote down for each.
2. Make a list of prototype conversations that might help you answer these questions.
3. Make a list of prototype experiences that might help you answer these questions.
4. If you are stuck, and if you have gathered a good group, have a brainstorming session to come up with possibilities. (Don't have a team? Try mind mapping.)
5. Build your prototypes by actively seeking out Life Design Interviews and experiences.

7

How Not to Get a Job

Steve Jobs and Bill Gates never wrote résumés, went to career fairs, or struggled over achieving the perfect tone, in the perfect first sentence, of the perfect cover letter. Perfection doesn't play a role in life design, and there is certainly nothing perfect about the standard American model that 90 percent of job seekers use to go about looking for a job—a technique that some say has a success rate of less than 5 percent. That's right, 90 percent of us are using a method that might only work 5 percent of the time.

Kurt had just completed a two-year fellowship after getting his master's in design in our program at Stanford—on top of one he already had from Yale in sustainable architecture—when he and his wife, Sandy, discovered their first baby was on the way. They decided to relocate from Silicon Valley to Atlanta, Georgia, to start their family near Sandy's folks. Kurt was finally ready for all those shiny degrees to go to work and provide him a career that he could love and that would pay the bills. Kurt knew how to think like a designer, but when he first arrived in Georgia, he felt he needed to prove to himself (and to his wife and his in-laws) that he was serious about landing a job—and fast. So he got busy. He did his homework. He carefully found job postings in the area that fit his résumé well. He identified the most viable openings and submitted thirty-eight job applications, along with his impressive résumé and thirty-eight individually crafted cover letters.

He should have been beating the recruiters away with a stick and having more job offers than he could count, but it didn't work that way. Out of his thirty-eight applications, Kurt received terse rejection e-mails from eight companies and never heard anything at all from the other thirty. Eight nos and thirty nothings. No interviews, no offers, no follow-up calls. He was discouraged, disheartened, and more than a little concerned about how he was going to support his new baby when she arrived. And this was a guy educated at Yale and Stanford. Where does that leave the rest of us?

Kurt's first approach is what most people do—what we call the standard model of job seeking. You look for a job listing on the Internet or a corporate website, read the job description, decide whether that's the "perfect" job for you, submit your résumé and cover letter, and wait around for a hiring manager to call you for an interview. And you keep waiting.

And waiting.

Still waiting.

The problem is that 52 percent of employers have admitted that they respond to fewer than half of the candidates that apply.[1]

This standard model fails so much of the time because it is a model based on the mistaken idea that your perfect job is out there waiting for you.

Mining the Internet

The idea that somehow the Internet is the be-all and end-all when it comes to looking for a job has gotten a lot of traction, but it's yet another dysfunctional belief. This particular dysfunctional belief leads to a lot of frustration, with a side dish of demoralization.

Most great jobs—those that fall into the dream job category—are never publicly listed. The most interesting start-up jobs—at the companies that will someday be the next Google or Apple—are not listed on the Internet before they are filled. Companies with fewer than fifty employees and no human-resource departments are often exciting places to work, but they don't regularly post jobs. Large companies typically post their most interesting jobs internally only, invisible to most job seekers. Many other jobs are not listed until an attempt has been made to fill them through word of mouth or social networks. You don't find the great jobs on the Internet. No matter what your cousin's friend's brother told you about how he found his job.

When you are job hunting on the Internet, it takes an inordinate amount of time to craft a good cover letter, modify your résumé so it fits a particular job description, and manage and keep track of dozens and dozens of online applications. And after all that time and hard work, all you hear back is a whole lot of silence. Deafening silence. Positive feedback is so infrequent with Internet job-hunting that an already unpleasant activity (looking for a job) gets even more so. Using the Internet as your only job-finding method is nothing short of masochistic.

We don't recommend the Internet as your primary job-finding

method, but there are thousands of jobs listed there every week. If you insist on trying to generate job options by mining the postings on the Internet, we have a few insider tips for you to improve the chances that your Internet search will be productive.

Understanding Job Descriptions

We have to give the hiring managers of the world some credit here; they all have good intentions. It's just that the process doesn't work very well. Since advertising, interviewing, and hiring are repeated hundreds of times a year in average mid- to-large-sized companies, they can't be allowed to take too much time. No one wants to miss out on a good candidate, so companies post jobs on the Internet with fairly generic descriptions, looking for as many applications as possible. And remember, all of this hiring activity occurs in addition to the hiring manager's regular job assignment, so listing jobs accurately often doesn't get the time and focused attention it deserves.

How many times have you thought, "My résumé is a perfect fit for this job description!"? So you applied, only to get nothing back, not even an acknowledgment that they have your résumé? If you understand a couple of things about this process from an insider's point of view, it will make more sense and hurt a little less.

1.   **The job description on the website is typically not written by the hiring manager or someone who really understands the job.**

2. The job description almost never captures what the job actually requires for success.

To show you what we mean, let's take apart some components borrowed from or inspired by actual job descriptions that we pulled from the Internet. Most listings will have two or three sections that try to describe what the company is looking for.

Section 1: The Setup

This is the header of the job description, which often contains something like this

Company X is looking for a candidate (for job X) with the following:

- **Good written and verbal communication skills**
- **Strong analytical skills**
- **Excellent business planning and reporting skills**
- **Highly motivated and creative**
- **Demonstrated ability to juggle competing priorities and move quickly**
- **Strong initiative, bias for action, and a meticulously high attention to detail**
- **Innovative and market-savvy**
- **A passion for customers**

These job qualifications are so generic that they really tell you nothing at all about the job. They are the attributes (not skills) of any good employee. They are also almost impossible to screen for by just looking at a résumé.

Section 2: Skills

The generic attributes section is typically followed by a section with a ridiculously detailed list of very specific educational requirements and skills.

Excellent candidates for the job will have the following experience:

- **A bachelor's, master's, or Ph.D. with ten years' experience (doing exactly what we do in our company)**
- **Five to ten years of experience with (some obscure legacy software program that we still use)**
- **Three to five years of experience with (some obscure job-specific task that only people who work here know how to do)**

This part of the job description is always based on the skills of the previous jobholder; it's historical. It does not take into account the possibility that the job will change in the future, or that the very specific knowledge required would be irrelevant in six months, when the company changes from one software platform to another. Nor does it account for the fact that office procedures and other methods of operation constantly evolve in any healthy, growing company.

Section 3: "What Makes the Candidate Special"

Wait, we're not done yet. Our favorite part of job descriptions is where the overworked HR person or office manager writing this thing accidentally decides to let the truth sneak into the description and adds qualifications like

- **This role is not for the faint of heart, and only those with a proven and successful track record should apply.**

We call this the "You'd have to be crazy to take this job" qualifier. It really means "This job really sucks, and only people who have a proven track record of surviving sucky jobs should apply."

- **Looking for: superheroes with the ability to produce ridiculous amounts of work on ludicrously tight deadlines**.

This "superhero" qualifier should be read as "This job is impossible, and no one can do it."

- **On top of your ability to create elegant and inspiring solutions, you are insightful and persuasive when analyzing and discussing strategies with colleagues.**

We call this the "wishful thinking" qualifier. We've never met a job seeker who didn't think he or she was insightful and persuasive, elegant and inspiring. It's nice that we all think of ourselves this way, but it's not much help when you're screening candidates.

Again, we didn't make any of this up. We took these words right off of major corporate job websites. And we don't think this is a very smart way for companies to act—it's unlikely that these job descriptions will attract only the best-qualified candidates. But, that said, there are ways to improve your chances of using Internet job listings to find a job when you know how these things are created.

Fit In Before You Stand Out

To get considered for an interview, your résumé has to end up on the top of somebody's pile. So job number one is to "fit in." This doesn't mean you should say anything about yourself that isn't true. It does mean that, if you want to be discovered, you need to describe yourself with the same words that the company uses. It also means that you don't want to talk about your amazing multidisciplinary skill set yet—it will only confuse the "fit" evaluation.

Most mid- to-large-sized companies that use the Internet to collect résumés scan them into an HR or "talent management" database. The hiring manager never sees the original. Your résumé will be "discovered" in a keyword search of the database, and the keywords used most often come from the job description. So, to increase you chance of being discovered, use the same words that they used in the first part of the job description.

The specific skills that are listed as required are important, but often not a deal maker or breaker. Remember, their descriptions are written from the point of view of the current job, not the future. If you have those specific skills, great; add them to your résumé, word for word. If you don't, list very specific skills that are similar. Find ways to describe those skills that might come up in a keyword search based on the job description.

Finally, in the "screening candidates" phase of the hiring process, people are looking for a skills match. Once you get to the interview, you have to be very careful to craft a good "fit" story. If you are trying out for a softball team and the softball manager needs a pitcher, that's what he's looking for. Not a catcher, not a right fielder. Now is not the time to talk about collecting baseball cards, winning baseball trivia contests, and your hobby of making baseball-shaped cakes. You just talk about pitching. In the screening phase of the process, do not talk about your other amazing talents or bring up skills you possess that aren't part of the job description. You will come across as unfocused. You might sound like you are not interested in the job. Worse yet, you come across as a bad listener, because you will be perceived as answering a question that hasn't been asked. There is a time to "stand out" later in the process, but if you do it in the beginning, you will be ejected from the candidate pool.

Here is a summary of our tips to make your Internet job search strategy more effective:

Tip 1: Rewrite your résumé using the same words used in the job posting. Say "good written and verbal communication skills," not "I'm a good writer and I communicate well"; say "passion for customers," not "customer-centric attitude." You will improve your chance of being discovered in a keyword search. And be generous; now is not the time for modesty. After all, who isn't "highly motivated" and "creative"?

Tip 2: If you have a specific skill that is posted as

required, put it in your résumé exactly the way it is written in the Internet posting. If you don't have that skill, find a way to describe your skill set that uses the same words that will be found in a keyword search.

Tip 3: Focus your résumé on the job as described. Even if the job description isn't very accurate, this will increase the chance that your résumé will show up in a search. Then focus on the skills that you can offer the company, using their words as often as possible. Focus on what you can do for them, not on why this job works for you. Do not appear to be a generalist or a multidisciplinary person on your résumé or in the first interview. Just focus on answering their needs. Once you have reassured them that you have the skills required, you can move on to impress them with your depth. That's how you "stand out."

Tip 4: Always bring a fresh, nicely printed copy of your résumé to an interview. This will probably be the first time anyone will see the care you put into designing the darn thing.

There are a couple of other things to be aware of if you want to practice safe surfing on the Internet for jobs. Knowing about these can save you hundreds of hours of fruitless job hunting.

The Super–Job Description Syndrome

In our experience, it's quite common for people to post job qualifications that the folks currently in the job can't possibly meet.

This managerial wishful thinking is a syndrome affecting most of corporate America. The process goes something like this:

Jane (the employee who quit) was a great program manager, but, boy, I wish she had been better at X, Y, and Z. Now that she's gone, let's post a job for a "Super Jane" and list all the things that Jane used to do, and all the things we wish she had done, and hope for the best.

The super–job description is posted, résumés are collected from keyword searches, and candidates are screened by phone. Interviews are scheduled, and candidate after candidate is interviewed and rejected because he or she is not a "Super Jane." This is especially true since no one who fits the new job description will work for what they used to pay Jane. Interview processes like these are essentially broken—they burn out both the interview team and the candidates, and nobody gets hired.

As a job seeker, you want to find out as soon as you can if you're involved in an interview process like this.

One way is to do some research and find out how long the job has been posted. In a good labor market, a job posting should never be open for more than four weeks (six at the max).

Another is to find out how many people have already been interviewed. Both data points will give you a sense of what's going on behind the scenes. It's surprisingly not hard to find this out. Just ask one of the people on the interview team. If they are in this situation, they know something is wrong, they are frustrated, and they will probably tell you. And they'll probably confess to wanting to leave the company. This happens more often than you think!

In our experience, if more than eight people have been through the wringer and no decisions have been made, the hiring process is probably broken. This is a sign that the company may not be a great place to work, and you might want to walk quickly to the exit.

The Phantom Job Listing Syndrome

This is another thing to be on the lookout for. Many companies have a rule that before they can hire someone for a job they have to post the job description, purportedly to make sure that the best candidates are identified and hired. But many times managers have already selected an internal or external candidate they want to hire for the job. Being good at getting around corporate bureaucracy, they write up a very detailed job description—one that matches their candidate's résumé exactly—post the "phantom" job description, wait the required two weeks, do a few cursory interviews, and then hire the person they wanted all along. Since the job description was written to match the preselected candidate's résumé, the hiring manager can "prove" that he or she hired the most qualified person.

These "job" openings never really existed at all. But you may have seen one and applied, thinking it was real, and then never heard back from the company. Or, worse, they wasted your time with a cursory interview and then never followed up. One way to tell if this is happening is to find out how quickly job descriptions churn on a company's website. If they are coming and going every week or two, this might be the reason.

Warning: Cool Companies and False Positives

There's a particular issue to be aware of if you're applying to a cool company—a hot, growing, successful company that everyone wants to work for. Here in Silicon Valley, it's Google, Apple, Facebook, and Twitter—you may have heard of them. Cool companies can be found in all healthy industries; you probably know the ones in the industries you're attracted to. The problem is an oversupply of not only qualified candidates but really great candidates. These companies have far more top candidates than they have openings. Consequently, cool companies have no fear whatsoever about being able to hire terrific people. Their only fear is that they might hire a bad candidate. If a company erroneously concludes someone is a good candidate when the person is really just average, that's a "false positive"—and it's a hiring nightmare.

A bad hire is incredibly expensive and painful. It's tough to fire people these days (employment litigation is at an all-time high), and after you do, you still have to go through the whole search process again, and the important work you hired them for isn't getting done, and schedules are slipping, and money is being lost, and . . . The list goes on and on. Companies will do anything they can to avoid false positives in hiring. This includes being quite tolerant of false negatives—misperceiving that someone's a bad candidate when the person is actually a great candidate. Mistakenly letting a great candidate go doesn't cost a cool company a thing: they have plenty of spare great candidates, so letting a few spill on the ground is a much better mistake to make than hiring a bad candidate. Therefore, cool companies' hiring processes are sometimes rather draconian. Great people get rejected frequently, and often with no idea why. It could happen to you. These companies often *can* get people who really are almost *exactly* like what their crazy job listing is asking for (I know we said that doesn't happen in reality—but cool companies distort that reality). So, if you are at all out of alignment with their desired candidate profile, or even just a few days late getting into line, you may have no chance, even if you're a great candidate who would be a terrific hire. They don't care. They don't have to. It's not meanness—it's just a smart business decision, grown of necessity caused by their popularity and success.

This is a gravity problem: you can't do anything about it. If you want to go after one of these cool companies, you're just going to have to play their game by their rules and hope you've got what it takes to win. Remember, they do want to hire great people, and the company may be a great place to work if you can just pull it off. If you want to work at a cool company, you really do want to get connected to people inside that company, using the prototyping conversations we've discussed. A personal connection can help you greatly. You'll still have to go through the hiring process, but you'll have some help. We're not saying you shouldn't try—many employees at cool companies love their work, so it may be worth the effort. But be brutally honest with yourself about your chances, and *caveat emptor.*

The Way It Should Be

One thing that you may have noticed is the conspicuous absence of job descriptions that sound like this:

- **Looking for candidates who would like to connect their Workview to their Lifeview**
- **Looking for candidates who believe that good work is found through the proper exercise of their signature strengths**
- **Looking for candidates with high integrity, the capacity to learn quickly, and high intrinsic motivation; we can teach you all the rest**

In our perfect world, that's how it would work.

So here's how it goes: Companies post these tortured job descriptions that describe almost nothing useful about the job to the potential employee. Then they surround those descriptions with ridiculous comments about superheroes and courage. None of the job descriptions we found when we went looking on the Internet seemed to address any of the issues we've been discussing. They didn't speak to the deeper issues of why we work or what work is for. It's a wonder that anyone would want to apply for one of these jobs.

Remember, life designers do not work on gravity problems. We are not going to "fix" Internet job postings. But don't worry. Even though the job descriptions posted on the Internet are pretty much useless, they still represent a potential starting point in your conversation with the institution they represent.

Awareness is key to life design, and this is true especially when you are designing your career. If you are aware of the process involved in hiring, in writing job descriptions, in reading résumés, in interviewing (from the employer's perspective), your success rate in getting a job offer goes way up. Empathy is a crucial element in design thinking, and having empathy—and understanding—for the poor hiring manager buried under a sea of résumés will help you know how to design a more effective job hunt. Effectiveness in getting hired involves a simple yet important design reframe.

Dysfunctional Belief: *You should focus on your need to find a job.*
Reframe: *You should focus on the hiring manager's need to find the right person.*

The bottom line is that there is no perfect job that you perfectly fit, but you can make lots of jobs perfect enough.

8

Designing Your Dream Job

Dysfunctional Belief: *My dream job is out there waiting.*
Reframe: *You design your dream job through a process of actively seeking and co-creating it.*

So, if your dream job isn't on the front doorstep waiting for you when you come home, where do you find it? First of all, let's clarify that there is no dream job. No unicorns. No free lunch. What you can find out there are lots of interesting jobs in worthwhile organizations populated by dedicated and hardworking people trying to do honest work. There are good jobs in good places with good co-workers, and there are at least a couple of those good jobs that you can make close enough to perfect so you can really love them. Those are the "dream jobs" we can help you find, but almost all of them are invisible to you now, because they're part of the hidden job market.

As we said earlier, we don't recommend mining the Internet for a job. In fact, in the United States only 20 percent of all the jobs available are posted on the Internet—or posted anywhere, for that matter. This means a full four out of five jobs that are available, are not available through the standard model of job hunting. It's a staggering number; no wonder so many people feel frustrated and rejected when job seeking.

How can you break into this hidden job market? Well, you can't. No one can. There is no such thing as breaking into the hidden job market. The hidden job market is the job market that's only open to people who are already connected into the web of professional relationships in which that job resides. This is an insider's game, and it's almost impossible to get inside that web as a job seeker. But it's quite possible to crack into the network as a sincerely interested inquirer—someone just looking for the story (not looking for the job). That's how this works. It is a wonderfully happy accident that the very best technique you can use to learn what kind of work you might want to pursue (prototyping with Life Design Interviews, as discussed in chapter 6) is exactly the best, if not only, way to get into the hidden job market in your field of interest, once you know what you want. Kurt—the one with master's degrees from Yale and Stanford, and thirty-eight carefully crafted applications with zero offers—was disheartened by his lack of success with traditional job-finding methods. Realizing it was time to apply design thinking to his job search, Kurt stopped applying for jobs and began conducting Life Design Interviews. He conducted fifty-six authentic prototype conversations with people he was genuinely interested in meeting. Those fifty-six conversations resulted in seven different high-quality job offers, and one dream job (the real kind, not the fantasy kind)—which he got. He now works full-time for a company where he has flexible hours, a short commute, decent money, and work that is meaningful to him in the field of environmentally sustainable design. And he got access to the opportunities that produced those seven offers *not* by asking for a job but by asking for people's life stories—fifty-six times.

Remember, all you're looking for from a Life Design Interview (functioning as a prototype conversation) is to learn about a particular kind of work or role to help you find out if you want, at a later date, to try to get a job doing that kind of work yourself. While conducting the conversation, you really are *not* after the job—you're after the story. "But wait a minute," you say. "You just told me how Kurt got seven offers out of his fifty-six Life Design Interviews. How'd that happen? How does getting the story turn into getting the job?" Good question. Important question. The answer is surprisingly simple.

Most of the time, the person talking to you does it for you. "Kurt, you seem very interested in what we do here, and from what you've said so far, it sounds like you have talents we could use. Have you ever thought of working someplace like this?"

More than half the time, when the approach we're recommending results in an offer, they initiate it. You don't have to. If they don't start it for you, you can ask one question that will convert the conversation from getting their story to pursuing a job.

"The more I learn about XYZ Environmental and the more people I meet here, the more fascinating it becomes. I wonder, Allen, what steps would be involved in exploring how someone like me might become a part of this organization?"

That's it. As soon as you ask, "What steps would be involved in exploring how someone like me might become a part of this organization?," Allen knows it's time to shift gears and start thinking critically about you as a candidate. It means he'll start using his judging brain, but that's okay. It's gotta happen sometime, so when the time is right—go for it.

Note that you don't say, "Wow—this place is great! Do you have any openings?" For the reasons already mentioned, the answer is probably "No." The "What steps would be involved in exploring . . ." question is open-ended (not yes or no) and invites possibilities far beyond just what's available today. And if you're asking it of someone like Allen, with whom you've established a connection and earned some regard, we hope he's going to give you a candid but supportive reply. In some cases, Allen may even say, "No, we don't have anything coming soon around here, but I think you might be a great fit in one of our partner companies. Have you met anyone at Green Space yet? I think you'd like what they're doing."

It happens. All the time.

By the way, in six of the seven places where Kurt received offers, he didn't have to ask about openings. He just got the stories of the people he was interviewing, and they asked him. All but one of the offers he got were for unlisted jobs—part of the hidden job market. The job that was listed was the one he ended up taking. But the listing wasn't posted publicly until after he'd already scheduled a Life Design Interview with the CEO, which went so well that, by the time it was posted, he had it wired.

Oh, and one more little tidbit about Kurt's story. The final interview at the company where he now works was with the five-person board of directors. Their first question was "Do you think you can be effective in establishing partner relationships within the sustainable architecture community here? After all, you've just moved to Georgia." Looking around the table, Kurt had the happy surprise of recognizing three of the five board members as people he'd already met over coffee. He answered, "Well, I've already successfully reached out to three of you. I'd be happy to keep doing that kind of outreach on behalf of this organization." Yeah—he nailed the interview. But before any of that, he had to do a lot of networking.

People: The Other World Wide Web

When Kurt really put his shoulder into the hard work of lining up lots of prototyping conversations, he had to reach out to all kinds of people to get connections and referrals to those whom he needed to meet. To get those referrals, Kurt had to "network." He had to reach out to his contacts, and their contacts, and he even had to reach out to strangers he'd identified online. Then he asked those people whom he should be talking to—whose stories he should be getting if he wanted to learn more about sustainable architecture in the Atlanta area. It was hard. It was not Kurt's favorite part of the process (actually, it's nobody's favorite part), but it worked. And it's absolutely necessary.

Now, a lot of people have an instant aversion to the term "networking." It conjures up images of slick, self-interested people manipulating others to get things they don't deserve, or hucksters pretending to care about someone just for the purpose of using that person to get to someone else. These negative images are powerful and reinforced by lots of characters in films and novels, as well as too many real people we've encountered or heard about. The good news is that, although these stereotypes are not without real-life examples, they are by far the minority. Let us see if we can make it easier for you by giving a different image of networking (a reframe).

Dysfunctional Belief: *Networking is just hustling people— it's slimy.*
Reframe: *Networking is just asking for directions.*

Think about the last time you were walking down the street in your city or town, and an unknown car pulled up slowly alongside you. The window rolled down, and the driver or passenger leaned toward you with an obvious look of distress. Now, depending on where you live, your first instinct may have been to duck and take cover, run screaming, or pull out your can of pepper spray, but for most of us the first inclination would be to offer help.

The person in the car is lost and asking you for directions to the nearest coffee shop, or freeway entrance, or amusement park, or antiques stores. What do you do? Well, most of us will give them directions if we can. We help them out. Perhaps they ask you a little about your town, other places they might want to visit, or they ask you what the service is like at the coffee shop you've directed them to. They leave, and you go on your way. How do you feel when they drive away with your directions and information? Do you feel used? Are you offended that they won't call you the next day or become your friend on Facebook, or that they care more about getting to the nearest coffee shop than they care about you? Of course not. You are not friends. You haven't entered into a relationship. What you do feel is great about having helped another human being. Multiple studies confirm this—most of us like being helpful. It's hard-wired into our DNA. We are social creatures, and helping one another is one of the things that makes us feel best.

Kurt didn't know his way around the sustainable architecture industry in Atlanta. You may not know your way around the nano-technology community in Hong Kong, or the craft beer crowd in Wichita, or the emergency-room nursing union in Seattle. What do you do? You ask a local for directions. Getting referrals to people whose stories would be useful to hear is just the professional equivalent of asking directions. So go ahead—ask for directions. It's. No. Big. Deal.

"Network" is more noun than verb. The point isn't to "do" network-*ing;* the goal is to participate in the network. Simply put, it just means to enter into a particular community that's having a particular conversation (such as sustainable architecture). Every domain of human endeavor is held together by a web of relation-ships between people. Real people. That web is the fabric that undergirds, contains, and holds together that part of society. The Stanford "network" that we are a part of holds Stanford together. The Silicon Valley "network" is the loose community of West Coast folk that allows tech entrepreneurship to flourish. Most individuals have both a professional network (of colleagues) and a personal network (of friends and family). The most common way for people to be introduced across professional networks is by referrals from personal networks. This isn't favoritism—it's just communal behavior. The use of personal or professional networks to initiate new people into a community's conversation is a good thing. The network exists to sustain the community of people getting the work done—and is the only way to gain access to the hidden job market.

Speaking of the World Wide Web, it turns out that networking is one place where the Internet really can transform your job search. Use the Internet not to get online job listings but to find and reach out to the people whose stories you want to hear. Bella, one of our students who graduated a few years ago, just called to tell us how happy she was, and how well this approach had worked for her. She had successfully figured out what she wanted to do (impact investing in the developing world) and designed her way to three great offers in that field including the one she accepted with a boutique firm she'd never heard of before—and it only took two hundred conversations to do it. Two hundred. In just six months. Really.

Bella reported that she was able to find and reach out to well over half of those two hundred by using Google and LinkedIn. Of course she did her homework on individuals and organizations and networked to obtain a personal referral whenever she could, but smartly leveraging her use of Internet tools made a huge difference. LinkedIn has utterly transformed our ability to find the people we're looking for. There are lots of books and online programs to teach you how to be effective using these tools (some of the best ones are offered by LinkedIn themselves). Use them. If you become a superstar at using LinkedIn and Google, the Internet can make a difference for you, and will no longer be the black hole into which you submit countless applications.

Focus on Offers—Not Jobs

Every year, the National Association of Colleges and Employers (NACE), a nonprofit established in 1956, compiles data on new college graduates and employment, such as the average salary of recent graduates, top skills employers are looking for, and also what graduates report as the top things they are looking for when it comes to a job. Guess what the first consideration was of the graduating class of 2014 when looking for a job.[1]

Nature of the work.

Salary and the friendliness of co-workers come in second and third, to complete this completely dysfunctional job-seeker trifecta.

The problem with this scenario is that there is no way to know the real "nature of the work" before you have gotten very close to actually getting the job. It's impossible. Since so many job descriptions are dysfunctional and inaccurate, most people rule out a job as not being "right" for them before they've even applied (and before they actually know what they're rejecting). It's a nasty chicken-and-egg problem that can severely shrink your potential opportunities. That's why the most important reframe when you are designing your career is this: you are never looking for a *job*, you are looking for an *offer*.

Dysfunctional Belief: *I am looking for a job.*
Reframe: *I am pursuing a number of offers.*

Now, this might not seem like a big distinction at first, but it is critical. It changes everything—from what jobs you consider, to how you approach cover letters and résumés, to how you interview, to how you close the deal and ultimately get the opportunities you're looking for. The biggest impact of this reframe is on your mind-set. It shifts you from being a person deciding whether or not you'd take this job (which you know nothing about) to being a person who is curious to find out what kind of interesting offer you might be able to find in that organization. It flips you from judging to exploring, from negative to positive—and that's a huge difference.

When you are looking for a job, your focus is on that job, and your behavior toward getting that job becomes centered around convincing the institution to hire you and conveying to them that this is your absolute, ultimate job, which you were born wanting. You have to convince the person or people in charge of filling that job that you and the job description are the perfect fit (match made in heaven, can't live without each other, have to be together or else). Since you don't really know much about the nature of the work, you have to fake your enthusiasm to make this process work. In other words, you either lie or you don't apply.

And nobody likes to lie.

But when you are looking for an offer rather than a job—when your goal switches from getting one job to getting as many job offers as possible—everything changes. You don't have to be deceptive. You can be genuinely curious about the job, because it is absolutely true that you would like the *opportunity* to evaluate an offer. It's not a matter of semantics; it's a matter of authenticity. When you reframe the job search into an offer search, you end up being more authentic, energetic, persistent, and playful while you pursue your next position or opportunity. And, ironically, this ends up making you more likely to get the offer. People don't hire résumés; they hire people. People they like. People who are interesting. And you know what types of people each of us is most interested in (whether it's as a potential date or a potential employee)—the ones who are most interested in us.

It goes back to curiosity—one of the most important life design mind-sets. Whether you are seeking your first job, changing careers, or choosing an encore career, you need to be genuinely curious. That's what prototyping conversations and prototyping experiences are all about: being open and curious about the possibilities. We call it pursuing latent wonderfulness. What this means is that you ask yourself, "Is there a 20 percent chance there's something interesting to me going on somewhere in this organization? Is there a 10 percent chance?" If the answer is yes, then don't you want to find it? Of course you do, and that desire to find it allows you to show genuine curiosity and a willingness to pursue the latent wonderfulness in an organization you may have unnecessarily dismissed outright as not being a fit for you.

You can't know the nature of the work until you've conducted further investigation, until you've pursued the offer. You can't know it from a faulty job description. You can't know it because of preconceived notions about what it's like to do *that* job, or work for *that* company.

You rarely know too much about a job before you get the offer, so pursue all the offers you can. All you need is the possibility that one of them might be a fit. That's it, just a possibility. And maybe someday, when the NACE does its annual study of what college graduates are looking for in a job, the number one thing isn't going to be the nature of the work. It's going to be latent wonderfulness. It's going to be more about possibility than preconception.

The Job Charming Fairy Tale

Kurt entered into genuine conversations, and he found a good job that he's been able to build into a great job. You can do the same. We know this is hard. We know this is a lot of work and is sometimes scary. But it's also incredibly interesting and is the only way we know to crack the hidden job market. To some degree, it's also a numbers game—the more connections you make, the more prototypes you run, the more opportunities will turn into offers.

Consider the alternatives.

Thirty-eight applications for zero offers.

Fifty-six conversations for seven offers and a great professional network.

Which approach do you like better? It's your call.

It is more than possible to use design thinking to get your first job, transform your current job, design your next job, and create a career that integrates your Workview and your Lifeview. In fact, we recommend it, because there is no Job Charming coming to rescue you. The idea that your dream job already exists, fully formed, just waiting for you to find it, is a fairy tale.

You design your "really pretty terrific and surprisingly close to a dream" job the same way you design your life—by thinking like a designer, by generating options, by prototyping, and by making the best choices possible.

And by learning to live into those choices.

9

Choosing Happiness

Designing a career and a life requires not only that you have lots of options and good alternatives, as we have discussed; it also requires the ability to make good choices and live into those choices with confidence, which means you accept them and don't second-guess yourself. Regardless of where you've started, what stage of life and career you are in, how great or dire you perceive your circumstances to be, we would bet our last dollar that there is one goal you all have in this life you are designing:

Happiness.

Who doesn't want to be happy? We want to be happy, and we want our students to be happy, and we want you to be happy.

In life design, being happy means you *choose* happiness.

Choosing happiness doesn't mean you should click your heels together three times while wishing to go to your happy place. The secret to happiness in life design isn't making the right choice; it's learning to choose well.

You can do all the work of life design—ideating and prototyping and taking action—all leading to some really cool alternative life design plans, but this doesn't guarantee you will be happy and get what you want. Maybe you'll end up happy and getting what you want, and maybe you won't. We say "maybe" because being happy and getting what you want are not about future risks and unknowns or whether you picked the right alternatives; it's about how you choose and how you live your choices once they're made. All of your hard work can be undone by poor choosing. Not so much by making the wrong choice (that's a risk, but, frankly, not a big one, and usually one you can recover from) as by thinking wrongly about your choosing. Adopting a good, healthy, smart life design choosing process is critical to a happy outcome. Many people are using a choosing model that cuts themselves off from their most important insights and actually prevents them from being happy with their choices after they've been made. We see it all the time, and studies agree: many people guarantee an unhappy outcome by how they approach this all-important design step of choosing.

Dysfunctional Belief: *To be happy, I have to make the right choice.*
Reframe: *There is no right choice—only good choosing.*

On the flip side, choosing well almost guarantees a happy and life-giving outcome, while setting you up for more options and a better future.

The Life Design Choosing Process

In life design, the choosing process has four steps. First you *gather and create* some options, then you *narrow down* your list to your top alternatives, then you finally *choose,* and then, last but not least, you . . . *agonize* over that choice. Agonize over whether you've done the right thing. In fact, we encourage you to spend countless hours, days, months, or even decades agonizing.

Just kidding. People can waste years agonizing over the choices they've made, but agonizing is a time suck. Of course we don't want you to agonize, and that is not the fourth step in the life design choosing process.

GATHER & CREATE ⇨ NARROW DOWN ⇨ CHOOSE ⇨ ~~AGONIZE~~

The fourth step in the process is to *let go* of our unnecessary options and *move on,* embracing our choice fully so that we can get the most from it.

GATHER & CREATE ⇨ NARROW DOWN ⇨ CHOOSE ⇨ LET GO & MOVE ON

We need to understand each of these choosing steps to appreciate the important difference between good choosing, which results in reliably happy outcomes and more future prospects, and bad choosing, which preconditions us for an unhappy experience.

Step 1: Gather and Create Options

Gathering and creating options is what we've been discussing throughout this book. Having good insights about yourself, exploring options about where to engage with the world, and prototyping experiences are the ways that your life design process generates ideas, alternatives, and viable options that you can pursue (all pursued, of course, with a curious mind-set in which you're looking for latent wonderfulness, and approached with a bias to action versus overthinking). We won't spend any more time on option generation here, other than to tell you (again) to write your Workview and Lifeview, to create mind maps, do your three Odyssey Plan alternatives, and prototype conversations and experiences. You can use these option-generating tools for any area of your life.

Step 2: Narrow Down the List

Some people feel they don't have enough (or any) options. Other people, and most designers, feel they've got too many. If you've got too few, then go back to all those suggestions we've already made (step one), and invest the time needed to cultivate more ideas and options. It may take weeks or months to build up a list you really like, which is just fine. After all, it's your life we're designing here, and this is not going to happen overnight.

Now, once you've got a hefty list of options, chances are that you're struggling with all the possibilities. You look over all your ideas and all the suggestions other people have given you and all the things you could possibly do with your life, and . . . it can feel overwhelming. You find yourself unable to choose—or at least unable to choose with confidence—so you figure you've done something wrong. You must not have done enough "homework" and understood your options well enough. "If only I had better information and a clearer picture of these options, I'd know which one to choose." And off you go to do more research, interviewing, and prototyping. And it doesn't work. It doesn't work because, even though not having enough information is sometimes a real problem, it's usually not the core issue. By the time most of us are getting close to an important decision, we've done our homework. We may not know everything there is to know—in fact, all our investigating actually makes clearer to us what we don't know than what we do know, so we're pretty sure more research would be helpful—but that's not it. If you're like most of us, then the reason your choosing process is stuck isn't about your knowledge—it's about the length of your list and your relationship with all those options. We can most easily make this point clear by looking at how people buy jam.

Professor Sheena Iyengar from the Columbia Business School is a psycho-economist who specializes in decision making. Her famous "jam study" was done using specialty jams in a grocery store. One week, the researchers set up a table in the store showing off six different specialty jams (with snazzy flavors like kiwi-orange, strawberry-lavender . . . you get the idea). Then they watched how the shoppers behaved—who stopped to look and, of those who stopped, who actually bought some jam. The first

week, with six jams on display, 40 percent of the shoppers stopped to check out the six jams and about a third of them bought one—about 13 percent of the shoppers.

A few weeks later, in the same store, with the same time frame, the researchers came back with twenty-four jams. This time, 60 percent of the shoppers in the store stopped by—a 50 percent increase over the six-jam display! But with twenty-four jams on display, only 3 percent of the shoppers bought one.

What does this research tell us? First, that we *love* having options ("Whoa! Twenty-four jams?! Let's check this out!!"), and, second, that we can't deal with too many of them ("Um . . . so many . . . can't decide; let's go get some cheese"). In fact, most minds can choose effectively between only three to five options. If we're faced with more than that, our ability to make a choice begins to wane—many more than that and our ability to choose completely freezes. It's just the way our brains are wired. We're attracted to having alternatives, and our modern culture almost idolizes options for their own sake. Get lots of options! Keep your options open! Don't get locked in! We hear this sort of thinking all the time, and it seems to make sense, but there absolutely can be too much of this good option thing. When you toss in the Internet and the fact that we can now be made aware of seemingly every idea and activity on the planet after a subsecond Google search, most of us are suffering a pandemic attack of too many options.

The key is to reframe your idea of options by realizing that if you have too many options, you actually have none at all. If you get frozen in front of your daunting list of possibilities, then, in fact, you have no options. Remember that options only actually create value in your life when they are chosen and realized. We often teach our students that when an option grows up it becomes a choice. So, when you've got twenty-four jam options, you actually have zero options. Once you understand that, in choice making, twenty-four equals zero (and, boy, is it hard to believe when you love your options and worked so hard to find and come up with them), then you are free to take the next step: narrowing down.

So what exactly do you do with too many options? Simple. Get rid of some. First, if it turns out that a lot of your options group together into categories, you can break your list down into smaller sublists. That may help you get to your top contender for each option type. But eventually you'll be in that overwhelmed-by-too-many-options place and have to get rid of a bunch of those jams. How? Just cross them off your list.

If you've got a list of twelve options, cross out seven, then rewrite your list with just the remaining five on it, and go to step three.

Most of our students and clients freak out at this idea.

"You can't just cross options off!"

"What if I cross out the wrong one?"

We understand. But we're not kidding—you just cross them off. Remember, if you've got too many options, you really don't have any, so you've got nothing to lose. And you won't cross off the wrong one. We call this the Pizza-Chinese Effect. We've all experienced it. Ed sticks his head in your office and says, "Hey, Paula—we're going out for lunch. Wanna come?"

"Sure!"

"We're choosing between pizza and Chinese food—got a preference?"

"Nah—whatever's good!"

"Okay—we're getting pizza."

"No, wait. I want Chinese!"

In that situation, when you gave your first answer ("whatever's good"), you thought you meant it. You didn't know that you had a preference until an unwanted decision occurred as a *fait accompli*. Only after the choice was named did you become aware of your preference. So you really can't lose when you're shortening your list of options. If you cross out the wrong ones, you'll know afterward. You may have to go as far as crossing out seven of the twelve and rewriting that new, clean list of just five before you realize it, but if it's wrong, you'll know. Trust us when we tell you that you can trust yourself. And if you find that you can't choose among the five alternatives, either, check which of two very different reasons might apply. The most common reason is that you're still just in agony over losing those seven other options and are refusing to let them go. If that's the case, then do whatever you need to in order to shorten your list. Burn the list of the seven you rejected, put it all down for a day or two, then come back to your list of five later and treat that list as *the* list (not the *shortened* list), but do eventually get going. If, however, you can't act on your list of five because you really can't find any preferences or meaningful distinctions between them, then—you win! You have just discovered that you've got a can't-lose situation on your hands. That means that all five options are strategically worthwhile for you, with no real distinctive difference. They will all work for you, which leaves you to choose based on secondary considerations (the drive is easier, the logo is cool, the story will be sexier at cocktail parties).

The point is that you want to leave the store with some jam.

Step 3: Choose Discerningly

Now—once you've done the preliminary work of gathering and narrowing down (and, yes, you do want to gather lots of options up front, choice overload notwithstanding, because then you're choosing from the best list), the hard part starts: actually choosing.

To choose well, we need to understand how our brains work

in the process of choosing. Where do good choices come from, and how do we know when we know? Fortunately, we are now living in an era of unprecedented progress in brain research, and we're learning tons about how we think, remember, and decide. In 1990, John Mayer and Peter Salovey wrote the seminal scholarly article launching the concept of "emotional intelligence" and proposing that, in achieving success and happiness, our "EQ" was as important as, and in many situations more important than, our "IQ," measuring our cognitive intelligence.[1] In 1995, the *New York Times* science writer Dan Goleman popularized their ideas in his book *Emotional Intelligence,* and a cultural phenomenon was launched.[2] "Emotional intelligence" is a phrase everybody has heard and has some regard for, but few people fully understand what it means, and fewer still are learning and benefiting from it.

It turns out that the part of the brain that is working to help us make our best choices is in the basal ganglia. It's part of the ancient base brain, and as such does not have connections to our verbal centers, so it does not communicate in words. It communicates in feelings and via connections to the intestines—those good old gut feelings. The memories that inform this choice-guiding function in our brains Goleman refers to as the "wisdom of the emotions"; by this he means the collected experiences of what has and hasn't worked for us in life, and what we draw upon in evaluating a decision. Our own wisdom is then made available to us emotionally (as feelings) and intestinally (as a bodily, gut response). Therefore, in order to make a good decision, we need access to our feelings and gut reactions to the alternatives.

Remember that default response to being stuck on a decision: I must need more information! We can now see that that is exactly what we *do not* need. It is our too-noisy brains, talking at us constantly as they try to cogitate our way to a good decision, that are getting in the way of connecting to our gut feelings on the decision. It is very important to have good information available—to do lots of homework and take lots of notes and make spreadsheets and comparisons and talk to experts, et cetera, et cetera, et cetera. But once that work is done—led by the prefrontal cortex of the brain, which runs the executive functions of coding, listing, and categorizing—we need access to that wisdom center where our well-informed emotional knowing can help us discern the better choices for us.

We define discernment as decision making that employs more than one way of knowing. We mostly use cognitive knowing—all that good, objective, organized, informational kind of knowing—the sort of knowing that gets you A's in school. But we also have other ways of knowing, including the affective forms of intuitive, spiritual, and emotional knowing. Add to those both social knowing (with others) and kinesthetic knowing (in our bodies). An incredibly skilled therapist friend of Dave's always knew when she was getting to the important issue with a client: her left knee would start to ache. She didn't know why it was her left knee, but over years of attentive practice she came to trust what her knee had to tell her. Because she learned to listen to her knee, she was able to make better decisions and better serve her clients by having access to that awareness.

The key to step three is to make discerning decisions by applying more than one way of knowing, and in particular not applying just cognitive judgment by itself, which is informed but not reliable on its own. We aren't suggesting making only emotional decisions, either. We all have examples of emotions getting people in trouble (though usually those are impulse emotions, and that's a very different thing), so we're not saying to swap your brain for your heart or your gut. We're inviting you to integrate all your decision-making faculties, and to be sure you make space so your emotional and intuitive ways of knowing can surface in the process.

In other words, don't forget to listen to your knee or your gut or your heart, too.

Doing this requires that you educate and mature your access to and awareness of your emotional/intuitive/spiritual ways of knowing (or however you may name these affective aspects of our shared humanity). For centuries, the most commonly affirmed path to such maturity has been that of personal practices such as journaling, prayer or spiritual exercises, meditation, integrated physical practices like yoga or Tai Chi, and so on.

We don't have the space, nor do we claim the expertise, to coach you on forming your set of personal practices, but we do encourage you to do so. The reason practices work to give you better access to your best wisdom in discerning a good decision relates precisely to the nature of such insights. Emotional, intuitive, and spiritual forms of knowing are usually subtle, quiet, and even shy. Rarely do people get access to their deepest wisdom by rushing around a few hours before a deadline and talking a lot or surfing the Web. It's a slower, quieter thing. Practices are just that—practice. We both practice regularly, month in and month out—especially during our off season, when there's no pressure to perform and we can focus on just doing the practice and gaining strength and balance. The time for gaining maturity by practice isn't during the playoffs, when things are stressful and demanding. Decision making is stressful, so the best time to prepare for good choosing is when there's no choice at stake. That's when you can invest in your emotional intelligence and spiritual maturity so that those muscles are strong and trained when it's decision or game time.

The best time to get ready for step three is months or years before the choosing. That means the best time is right now—today is the best day to start making that investment.

Here's one specific technique you can try that emphasizes accessing the wisdom of your emotions: grok it.

Grokking

In his 1960s sci-fi classic *Stranger in a Strange Land,* Robert Heinlein invented the word "grok" to describe a way of knowing that Martians employ. It means to understand something deeply and completely, so much so that you feel you've become one with it. Because of its rarity, Martians don't just understand what water is or drink water—they grok it. Now grok has entered more common cultural use; "I grok that" is sort of like "I get that," only more so. It's "I get that" on steroids.

When you finally get down to making a choice from your narrowed-down list of alternatives, and you've cognitively evaluated the issues, and emotionally and meditatively contemplated the alternatives, it may be time to grok it. To grok a choice, you don't think about it—you become it. Let's say you've got three alternatives. Pick any one of them and stop thinking about it. Choose to think for the next one to three days that you are the person who has made the decision to pick Alternative A. Choice A is your reality right now. When you brush your teeth in the morning, you do so having chosen A. When you sit at a red light, you're waiting to proceed toward your destination related to living in Alternative A. You may or may not actually *say* things to other people about this—such as "Oh yeah, I'm moving to Beijing in May!"—because such statements will cause confusion later. But you get the idea: you'll just live in your head as the person *in an Alternative A reality.* You are not thinking *about* Alternative A from your current reality as a struggling choice maker. You are living calmly as one who has chosen A. After one to three days of this (how long is up to you and a matter of taste), then take at least a day or two off to be your regular self and reset. Then do the same thing with Alternative B, then another reset break, then Alternative C. Then one more reset break and, finally, a thoughtful reflection on what those experiences were like and which one of those people you might most like to be. This technique isn't guaranteed (no such techniques are), but you can see how the intention here is to allow your alternate forms of knowing—emotional, spiritual, social, intuitive—to have some room to express themselves to you, and thereby complement the evaluative, cognitive knowing, which, if you're like most of us, is the dominant form of thinking and choosing you rely on.

Step 4: ~~Agonize~~ Let Go and Move On

Before we discuss the step of letting go, it's important to address, at least briefly, why the fourth step is not "agonize." Agonizing looks like this:

"Did I do the right thing?"

"Am I sure this is really the best decision?"

"What if I'd done option four instead?"

"I wonder if I can go back and do it over?"

If you've no idea what we're talking about here, consider your-self unusually fortunate, thank your parents for good brain-chemistry DNA, and skip ahead. But if you're like most of us, these are familiar questions. We hear lots of groans of recognition when we say, "And the last step is . . . agonize about the decision over and over!" Those groans are a signal of our shared humanity in this experience of decision making. The reason we're agonizing is that we care about our lives and the lives of others. These deci-sions matter, and we want to do our best to give the future its best possible chance. We want to make good decisions, but of course we can't possibly know if we've done so right away: unknowns are always out there, and none of us can see the future accurately. So how do we beat this post-decision agony thing?

It turns out that our mind-set about how to make a good deci-sion is as important as which decision we make. It seems obvious that the best way to be happy with a choice is to make the best choice. Simple enough—except it's impossible. You can't make "the best choice," because you can't know what that best choice was until all the consequences have played out. You can work on making the best choice you can, given what's knowable at the moment, but if your goal is "make the best choice," you won't be able to know if you've done it. Your inability to know that keeps you focused on whether or not you did the right thing, and keeps you rehearsing the alternatives not chosen: this is called agoniz-ing. And all that rehashing drains satisfaction with the choice you did make and distracts you from getting energetically ahead on the choice you have made.

Dan Gilbert at Harvard has looked at this area and demon-strated the effect *letting go* of your options has, in a study evaluat-ing how people made decisions about different Monet art prints.[3]

He asked people to rank five different Monet prints according to their preference, numbering them from one to five. Whichever prints the subjects ranked numbers three and four he said the experimenters happened to have spare copies of and were letting subjects take one home with them. Of course, most of the people took the one they had ranked number three. Then, interestingly, the experimenters told some of the people that they could swap the one they took for the other one later if they wanted to, and the other people were told that whatever print they took home was it—no swapping.

After a few weeks, the experimenters checked back with the subjects. The people who had been told they could swap their prints—even though they had not done so—were less happy with their choices than the people who had chosen the exact same prints but had been told the choice was irreversible. It turns out that reversibility is not conducive to establishing reliable happiness with a decision. Apparently, just the invitation to reconsider and "keep your options open" makes us doubt and devalue our choice.

But wait . . . it gets worse. In his book *The Paradox of Choice,* the researcher Barry Schwartz informs us that this nasty little feature of how our brains handle decisions goes even further.[4] When we make a decision in the face of many options, or just while perceiving that there are lots of other options that we don't even know about, we are less happy with our choice. The problem here is not just the options we had and didn't pursue (the options we "keep open")—it's that mountain of options we never even had time to check out. The perception that there are gazillions of possibilities that may have been great but that we never got to is a powerful force against being at peace with our choice making; even if we don't know what it was, *there must have been a better option out there, and we missed it.* In the Internet-powered, globalized world, there are always a gazillion options, so we are now more capable of being unhappy with our choices than any generation in history has been.

Yay for us!

The key is to remember that imagined choices don't actually exist, because they're not actionable. We're not trying to live a fantasy life; we're trying to design a real and livable life. If we burdened ourselves with knowing everything about our decisions and discovering every option possible (which, of course, you should do if you're going to make "the best choice"), we'd never decide. In life design we know that there are countless possibilities but aren't stymied by that fact. We revel in exploring a few possibilities, *then taking action by starting with a choice.* Only by taking action can we build our way forward. So let's get better and better at building by getting better and better at letting go of the options we don't need any longer. (And now you have the confidence to know that you can always get more options in the future, just the way you got these.) This is key to choosing happiness and being happy with our choices.

When in doubt . . . let go and move on.

It really is that simple.

We are not saying you pretend you don't know about the roads not taken, or that you will never again discover something halfway down the path and decide to back up and make a correction. What we are saying is that there is a smarter way to proceed, which will significantly enhance your ability to be successful in implementing your choices, and lead to happiness and satisfaction on the journey.

Do yourself the favor of getting lots of options, then culling the list down to a short and manageable size (five max); then make the best choice that you can, given the time and resources available to you, get on with it, and build your way forward. Note that if you're doing this with prototype iteration, you don't have too much at stake, and you will be able to adjust as you go, before you really reach a significant investment. And once you make a choice—then embrace your choice and go with it. When the questions that lead to agonizing creep into your head, evict the thoughts, and direct your energy into living well the decisions you've made. Pay attention and learn as you go, of course, but don't get caught with your eyes fixated on the rearview mirror of decision regret.

This letting-go step relies primarily on personal discipline. Keep your reframed understanding of decision making handy, and be sure to win the internal argument with yourself when you're tempted to rehash and ruminate. Put in place the support you need to stick with it—find a life design collaborator or team to help remind you why you made the choice or choices you did; make a journal entry about your decision, and reread it when you get confused. Find what works to enable yourself to enjoy your choices fully.

Dysfunctional Belief: *Happiness is having it all.*
Reframe: *Happiness is letting go of what you don't need.*

Letting Go by Grabbing On

Andy was a top premed student. Except he wasn't really a pre-med, he was a pre–public-health or pre–med-tech-entrepreneur student. Andy had two primary ideas about his future and one backup, all in response to the same big mission—fix health care.

Andy could see that the health-care system needed massive reform, with significant increases in preventive care and wellness management, if we were ever going to fix health care's disproportionate drain on the economy, and the inaccessibility of medicine to all but the wealthy. He thought there were two ways he could be most effective at making an impact. He could become an influential health-care public-policy adviser, or he could become a medical-technology entrepreneur. Though it was out of vogue among his friends to consider getting involved in government and the public sector, Andy could see that only the people adjusting the really big control dials on health care were going to be in a position to cause deep change. As far as medical technology, he knew there was a lot happening in that sphere, and new technology could spur behavior changes that could possibly get traction faster—since they moved at the speed of the marketplace, not politics.

His backup plan was to "just be a doctor." It sounded funny to say it that way, given how respected the noble role of physician is in our society, and especially in his Asian extended family—but that's how he always said it to himself. He wasn't being dismissive; he was being honest. His backup plan was an insurance policy in the event he couldn't find a way to make a wide societal impact and needed to redirect his efforts to a smaller playing field. He figured that an individual doctor certainly could make an impact within his practice, and possibly even in his local hospitals and region. Maybe that was a path to offering a shining example of what better health care could be.

Which way to choose? Actually, that wasn't the tough decision for him. Andy was convinced that the policy route was the most potentially impactful and interesting, so that's the path he was going to pursue. The tough choice was how to do it. Should he go right from undergraduate studies into a master's in public health (M.P.H.) and then right off to Washington? Or go to medical school and get his M.D. first—then get his M.P.H.? Andy knew that in the medical culture M.D.s are revered, and their counsel on all things medical bears much more weight than that of non-M.D.s. He didn't actually believe that getting an M.D. would make him a smarter or more effective policy maker, but he really wanted to make a difference and was willing to consider the eight to ten years it would take to enhance his credibility (four years to get an M.D., and four to six years from residency to licensing).

This was a tough decision for him to make. Ten years felt like an incredibly long time to wait to get started on what he wanted to do.

Andy kept going around and around in his head, but couldn't land on a choice that he felt good about. As soon as he'd decide to get his M.P.H. now and get started, he'd say, "But . . . if they don't listen to me, that head start doesn't do any good!" And as soon as he'd land on going to med school, he'd say, "But . . . ten years is just too long to wait—who knows what will happen by then?" Andy kept chasing his own thoughts in an endless circle. He said he felt as if his brain were stuck on a hamster wheel, squeaking around and around all night long.

Andy stopped thinking about the decision and grokked it. As he did so, he discovered that Med School Andy felt better than Just Policy School Andy. While walking around being the guy becoming a doctor, Med School Andy found himself feeling worried about those ten years, but then thinking, "Yeah—it's a long time. But I'm really committed to this goal of impacting health care. I know that the path I'm taking means I'm doing *everything I can* to prepare well and give it my best shot. The problems will still be huge a decade from now; I'm not going to miss it. I just don't think I could live with myself if I didn't do my best." By contrast, when the question about "What if no one pays any attention to me without an M.D.?" occurred to Just Policy School Andy, he didn't have a good answer; all he could do was feel lousy about it.

So he chose to go to med school and dedicate the next ten years to becoming a licensed M.D., almost solely in order to be a more credible policy maker in the future. Okay—choice made, job done. Right?

Wrong.

Andy still had to implement step four—to let go and move on. Andy quickly realized why we gave this name to step four. The secret to letting go is moving on. Merely letting go is an incredibly hard thing to do—some would say it's impossible. For example, right now, put anything in your mind's eye *except a blue horse.* Whatever you do—do not think about or see a blue horse. No spotted blue horse. No blue unicorn. No blue pygmy pony with a red-and-white striped saddle and a pink ribbon on its tail.

Please keep not seeing a blue horse for the next sixty seconds.

Okay, how did you do? If you're like everybody we've ever

worked with, you were stampeded by blue horses. That's the problem with letting go—it's more of an inaction than an action, and your brain just hates that, the same way nature abhors a vacuum. So the key to letting go is to move on and grab something else. Put your attention *on* something—not *off* something.

How was Andy going to let go of the worry and distraction that he was wasting a decade of his life? How was he going to let go of all those images of getting his M.P.H. in just two years and jogging the halls of Congress, becoming the hot new policy wonk in health care? Andy realized that the way out of it is into it, and asked, "How can I move on and move into becoming a doctor?"

As soon as he did that, Andy realized that his Med School Andy choice gave him his backup plan for free—becoming a doctor. He knew that medical students actually start doing medicine within the first few years of their training, and all the residency years are spent doing clinical work. What kind of specialties would be most relevant to health-care policy? What medical schools had the strongest ties to Washington and an affiliated M.P.H. program? What kind of care-providing institutions would teach him the most: A local clinic? A big hospital? Small towns? Cities? As soon as he began to embrace what his medical training could contribute and how he could make the most of it, he had tons of ideas and lots of interesting questions to pursue. By imagining his way into moving on, he gave his mind permission to let go. And he came up with lots of ways to have prototype conversations and prototype experiences related to health-care policy in his role as a medical student and a resident.

Andy was a star pupil.

No More Hamster Wheel

Designers don't agonize. They don't dream about what could have been. They don't spin their wheels. And they don't waste their futures by hoping for a better past. Life designers see the adventure in whatever life they are currently building and living into. This is how you choose happiness.

And, really, is there any other choice?

10

Failure Immunity

Imagine there was a vaccine that could prevent you from ever failing. Just one tiny shot, and your life would be guaranteed to go exactly as planned—nothing but smooth sailing and success after success, as far as your eye could see. An entire life without failure sounds pretty good, doesn't it? No disappointment, no setbacks, no trouble, and no loss or grief seems like a fine way to live to most of us. Nobody likes failure. It feels terrible—that horrible sinking sensation in the pit of your stomach, the heavy weight of defeat that can make your chest feel like it's being crushed.

Who doesn't want to be immune to failure?

Unfortunately, there's no vaccine, and it's impossible never to fail. But it is possible to be immune from failure. We don't mean you'll be able to avoid the experience of having things not work out the way you hoped for; but you can become immune to the large majority of negative feelings of failure that burden your life needlessly. If you use the ideas and tools that we've been talking about so far, you will reduce your so-called failure rate, which is great, but we're after something much more valuable than just failure reduction. We're after failure immunity.

We've been trying a lot of different things on the way to designing a life that is worth the living. Using the curiosity mind-set, we've gone out into the world and met some interesting people. We've radically collaborated with friends and family and prototyped some meaningful engagements with the world. And throughout this life design journey, we've gotten comfortable with the bias-to-action mind-set, and whenever we're in doubt, we know it's time to *do* something.

All along, you have been developing something positive psychologists like Angela Duckworth call perseverance or grit.[1] Duckworth's studies on grit and self-control demonstrate that grit is a better measure of potential success than IQ. Failure immunity gives you grit to spare.

It's important to think of ourselves as life designers who are curious and action-oriented, and who like to make prototypes and "build our way forward" into the future. But when you take this approach to designing your life, you are going to experience failure. In fact, you are going to "fail by design" more with this approach than with any other. So it's important to understand what "failure" means in our process, and how to achieve what we call failure immunity.

The fear of failure looms so large in people's experience of their lives. It seems to relate to a fundamental perception in the way people define a good or a bad life. She was a *success* (yay, good!). He was a *failure* (boo, bad!). When you look at it that way, no one wants to be a failure. We imagine that at our funerals there will be some external judge (or some imagined life tenure committee) who will pass judgment on whether we managed to succeed or ended up failing.

Fortunately, if you're designing your life, you can't be a failure.

You may experience some prototypes and engagements that don't attain their goals (that "fail"), but remember, those were designed so you could learn some things. Once you become a life designing person and are living the ongoing creative process of life design, you can't fail; you can only be making progress and learning from the different kinds of experiences that failure and success both have to offer.

Infinite Failure

We trust that you now understand that prototyping to design your life is a great way to succeed sooner (in the big, important things) by failing more often (at the small, low-exposure learning experiences). Once you've done this prototype-iteration cycle a number of times, you will really begin to enjoy the process of learning via the prototype encounters that other people might call failure. As an example, one day just before our large Designing Your Life class started, Dave made a big change to one of the teaching exercises for that day's class. He had an idea and just wanted to try something out. He didn't even have time to tell Bill, so Bill heard it at the same time as the students did. After Dave announced the (never before attempted) exercise and the students were working on it, Bill came over to Dave and said, "This is great! I love that you are willing to fail miserably in front of eighty students! I have no idea if this exercise is going to work, but I love how you're prototyping it!" Dave and Bill have come to trust the process of life design so completely that they don't ever have a conversation about the *right way* to run their classes. When you really get the hang of the design thinking approach, you end up thinking differently about everything.

This is the first level of failure immunity—using a bias to action, failing fast, and being so clear on the learning value of a failure that the sting disappears (and, of course, you learn from the failure quickly and incorporate improvements). By the way, that exercise in class went pretty well, and then we decided to jettison it anyway and keep the prior version of the exercise because it was more effective. What a success!

There's a whole other level of failure immunity that we call big failure immunity, which comes from understanding the really big reframe in design thinking. Are you ready? Designing your life is actually what life is, because life is a process, not an outcome.

If you can get that, you've got it all.

Dysfunctional Belief: *We judge our life by the outcome.*
Reframe: *Life is a process, not an outcome.*

We are always growing from the present into the future, and therefore always changing. With each change comes a new design. Life is not an outcome; it's more like a dance. Life design is just a really good set of dance moves. Life is never done (until it is), and life design is never done (until you're done).

The philosopher James Carse wrote an interesting book called *Finite and Infinite Games.*[2] In it he asserts that just about everything we do in life is either a finite game, one in which we play *by the rules* in order to win—or an infinite game, one in which we play *with the rules* for the joy of getting to keep playing. Getting an A in chemistry is a finite game. Learning how the world is put together and how you fit in it is an infinite game. Coaching your son to win the spelling bee is a finite game. Having your son come to trust that you love him unconditionally is an infinite game. Life is full of both kinds of games. (By games we don't mean something trivial or childish. In this context, it simply means how we act in the world and what importance we place on our actions.) Everyone is playing both finite and infinite games all the time. One kind is not better than the other. Baseball is a great game to play, but it doesn't work without rules and winners and losers. Love is an infinite game—when played well, it goes on forever, and everyone plays to keep it going.

So what does this have to do with life design? Just this: when you remember that you are always playing the infinite game of becoming more and more yourself and designing how to express the amazingness of you into the world, you can't fail. With the infinite-game mind-set, you are not just adept at failure reduction—you are truly failure-immune. Sure, you'll experience pain and loss or serious setbacks, but they won't make you less of a person, and you don't experience these setbacks as an existential "failure" from which you can't recover.

Being and Doing

For millennia, people have struggled with the difficulty of balancing our focus on ourselves as human *beings* (which is more prevalent in Eastern cultures) or as human *doings* (which is more prevalent in Western cultures). Being or doing? The real inner me, or the busy, successful outer me? Which is it? Life design thinks that's a false dichotomy. Since life is a wicked problem that we never "solve," we just focus on getting better at living our lives by building our way forward. This diagram is, we think, a better way to imagine the process:

When designing your life, you start with who you are (chapters 1, 2, and 3). Then you have lots of ideas (rather than wait and wait to have the idea of the century) and you try things out by doing them (chapters 4, 5, and 6), and then you make the best choice you can (chapter 8). As you do all this, including making choices that set you on one path for a number of years, you grow various aspects of your personality and identity that are nurtured and called upon by those experiences—you become more yourself. In this way, you energize a very productive cycle of growth, naturally evolving from being, to doing, to becoming. Then it all repeats, as the more-like-you version of you (your new *being*) takes the next step of *doing,* and so it goes.

All of life's chapters—both the wonderfully victorious and the painfully difficult and disappointing—keep this growth cycle going if we have the right mind-set. In this way of seeing and experiencing things, you're always succeeding at the infinite game of discovering and engaging your own life in the world.

And that mind-set is a great big dose of our version of the failure immunity vaccine.

Dysfunctional Belief: *Life is a finite game, with winners and losers.*
Reframe: *Life is an infinite game, with no winners or losers.*

Now, you may be thinking that this sounds good, but in the real world it's just not so simple. We do believe (and we've seen it in others and lived it ourselves) that you really can reframe failures in such a way that you transform setbacks and have a happier, more fulfilling life. This isn't just our own rehash of positive thinking; it's a design tool that's imperative to life design.

Failure is just the raw material of success. We all screw up; we all have weaknesses; we all have growing pains. And we all have at least one story in us of an occasion when we've reframed a particular failure, where we've changed our perspective, and have seen how a failure turned out to be the best thing that ever happened.

We all have our stories of redemption. A perfectly planned life that never surprises you or challenges you or tests you is a perfectly boring life, not a well-designed life.

Embrace the flaws, the weaknesses, the major screwups, and all the things that happened over which you had no control. They are what make life worth living and worth designing.

Just ask Reed.

Winning and Losing and Winning

Reed always wanted to be a class officer at school, so he started running for office as soon as he could, in fifth grade. He lost.

He ran in sixth grade—and lost again. He ran for office every year, often twice a year, and lost every single time. By the end of his junior year of high school, he'd run for one school office or another and lost thirteen times in a row. During his last year of high school, he decided to run one more time—for senior class president.

Over the years, Reed's parents watched with agony as the losses mounted up. After four or five losses, they would wince every time Reed announced, "I'm going to run again!" They were smart enough not to discourage him, but inside they wished he'd just let it go and stop the bleeding. They couldn't stand to see him going through all those failures. But Reed didn't mind. Oh sure, he hated losing—but he wasn't changing his mind. He knew that if he kept at, it he'd learn what he was doing wrong and eventually he'd win—or at least he'd learn a bit more. In his mind, failure was just part of the process. With each successive loss, losing got less painful, which allowed him to take risks to see if new approaches would work. It gave him the courage to try out for other things—sports, acting. Most of these didn't pan out, but a couple did. Though he was delighted with his successes, he would have been just fine even if he'd failed at those, too. Failing over and over freed him to focus his energies on running the best campaigns he could. Each failure was a lesson, so when he ran, he never worried about losing. When he finally won and became senior class president, he was thrilled, but the point isn't that he finally won—the point is how he kept running.

It turned out to be a more important lesson than he realized.

At twenty-two, to anyone who looked at him from the outside, Reed seemed finally to be winning at life. Boy Scout. Class president. Quarterback. Ivy League. Crew champion. When he graduated from college with a degree in economics, his life seemed set on a straight course for success followed by more success. He landed a job with a top firm and for the first few years, his new career was going great.

His job took him on the road often, and during a business trip to the Midwest, Reed noticed a strange lump just below his neck. He went to a clinic during his lunch break to check it out, and by the time he boarded his flight home three days later, a doctor has confirmed his worst fears: Hodgkin's disease, a cancer of the lymph nodes. When he got home, he immediately began chemotherapy.

Cancer at twenty-five was not part of Reed's life design. But it was now part of his life.

A lifetime of experience dealing with failure had paid off. Pretty quickly, Reed was able to accept the reality of his situation and put all his energies into getting better. He didn't get stuck asking, "Why me?" Nor did he believe he had failed at being healthy. He was too busy getting another campaign prepared—this time, a campaign to beat cancer—and then using it. For the next year, he wasn't advancing his economic consulting career, as he had planned; he was undergoing surgery, radiation, and chemotherapy. He was also learning, at a very young age, just how fragile life is.

When his cancer treatment was over and his cancer was in remission, Reed had no idea what to do next. Actually, he had one idea—one somewhat crazy idea. There was this little item on his Odyssey Plan that he hadn't begun to prototype: taking a year off from everything and being a ski bum. He was conflicted. An all-American boy on the fast track to success just doesn't take a year off to become a ski bum and get nothing done.

Reed, however, was not your average Boy Scout any longer. He had just fought a war with cancer, and even though he knew the smart plan was to go back to building his career, and he worried that an additional year of employment gap might ruin his résumé and therefore ruin his life, Reed decided he wanted to *live* his life, not just *plan* it.

He did some prototype conversations with businesspeople before he made his decision, because he wanted to learn how future hiring managers might look at that decision, and concluded that he could afford the risk, and that the kind of people he'd want to work with would view his post-cancer ski adventure as a demonstration of boldness rather than irresponsibility. As for how other people would see it—well, that was their problem. The point isn't primarily that Reed "succeeded in beating cancer," but that he was able to enjoy failure immunity during the process, which enabled him to direct his energy productively and to learn things he could use later. By turning his problem into an advantage, he was able to design the best life possible in the face of adversity. It beats the hell out of being despondently confused about why bad things happen.

The failure immunity he began learning in the fifth grade just kept coming in handy. A few years later, Reed decided to go for his dream job—working for a professional sports franchise, in particular an NFL team. Though he didn't have any family connections in that world, he had met an up-and-coming NFL executive while in college and had been slowly building a network into the sports world through prototype conversations. He made some overtures into the industry, looking for work. The worst thing that could happen was being rejected, but with rejection no longer scary to him, why not at least try?

When his attempts at an NFL job failed, he let go and quickly redirected his efforts into his next, alternative plan.

Over a year later, he finally got a chance to apply for a job negotiating player contracts for an NFL team. Up against dozens of other candidates, many of whom had industry experience, he made it down to the final two and lost—he didn't get the job. It really hurt, but, again, he quickly redirected his efforts into an alternative plan, and he got a job in financial management, working for a great company.

But he didn't give up on the pro team. Despite being rejected, he kept prototyping that career. He stayed in touch with the NFL executives and spent hundreds of hours building innovative sports analysis models, which he would show them every now and then. This was not the usual behavior of people who lost a job. And, yes, he was eventually hired by that same NFL team, for a better job than the one he had originally tried for.

He had worked there for about three years when he decided that pro sports wasn't really where he wanted to be—he "failed" again. So he moved on to a health-care start-up, secure in the knowledge that, if that didn't work out, the next thing—or, barring that, the thing after that—would.

Reed is now completely failure-immune. He's not protected from the personal pain and loss of failure, but he's immune from being misinformed by failure—he doesn't ever believe that he is a failure or that failure defines him, or, in fact, that his failures were failures. His failures educate him in just the same way that his successes do. He likes success better, but he'll take whatever he gets and just keep failing his way forward.

To meet Reed today is to meet what appears in every way to be a very successful and content young man. He's happily married, with a beautiful baby girl and an irrepressibly delightful three-year-old son. He's tall, good-looking, and healthy. He and his wife just bought their first house, and he's doing well at a great young company, working in genetic testing and health care. Reed is certainly enjoying all his recent success, but he doesn't think of it in those terms. He's mostly just grateful, and knows that how well it feels life is going is much more about his mind-set than his current level of success.

This is the real reason why Reed is winning at life.

Failure Reframe Exercise

It's easy for us to describe the lofty goal of attaining failure immunity, but getting there is another matter. Here's an exercise to help you do just that—the failure reframe. Failure is the raw material of success, and the failure reframe is a process of converting that raw material into real growth. It's a simple three-step exercise:

1. **Log your failures.**
2. **Categorize your failures.**
3. **Identify growth insights.**

Log Your Failures

Just write down when you've messed up. You can do this by looking back over the last week, the last month, the last year, or make it your All-Time Failure Hits List. Any time frame can work. If you want to build the habit of converting failures to growth, then we suggest you do this once or twice a month until you've established a new way of thinking. Failure reframe is a healthy habit that leads to failure immunity.

Categorize Your Failures

It's useful to categorize failures into three types so you can more easily identify where the growth potential lies.

Screwups are just that—simple mistakes about things that you normally get right. It's not that you can't do better. You normally do these things right, so you don't really need to learn anything from this—you just screwed up. The best response here is to acknowledge you screwed up, apologize as needed, and move on.

Weaknesses are failures that happen because of one of your abiding failings. These are the mistakes that you make over and over. You know the source of these failures well. They are old friends. You've probably worked at correcting them already, and have improved as far as you think you're going to. You try to avoid getting caught by these weaknesses, but they happen. We're not suggesting you cave in prematurely and accept mediocre performance, but we are suggesting that there isn't much upside in trying to change your stripes. It's a judgment call, of course, but some failures are just part of your makeup, and your best strategy is avoidance of the situations that prompt them instead of improvement.

Growth opportunities are the failures that didn't have to happen, or at least don't have to happen the next time. The cause of these failures is identifiable, and a fix is available. We want to direct our attention here, rather than get distracted by the low return on spending too much time on the other failure types.

Identify Growth Insights

Do any of the growth opportunity failures offer an invitation for a real improvement? What is there to learn here? What went wrong (the critical failure factor)? What could be done differently next time (the critical success factor)? Look for an insight to capture that could change things next time. Jot it down and put it to work. That's it—a simple reframe.

Here are some examples from Dave's almost endlessly long failure log.

Failure	Screwup	Weakness	Growth Opportunity	Insight
LISA's BDAY 1 WK. LATE !	X (OUCH!)			
LAST MINUTE BUDGET		X		
PHONE SURPRISE			X	START THE CALL WITH NEEDS & AGENDA
TERMITE THIEVES	X (BIG TIME)			

Dave did actually miss his daughter Lisa's birthday. By exactly a week. He doesn't remember this sort of thing well at all (a weakness), so he uses his calendar to remind himself. But one year he accidentally wrote it on the wrong week. He carefully planned a nice birthday dinner out with her—seven days after her birthday.

He managed to stay in the dark for the whole week by being on the road. Total screwup. Weird mistake. Not going to happen again. Another awful screwup was getting robbed. While the house was being fumigated for termites, Dave and his wife had to move out for three days, during which time thieves broke into the tented house and stole everything of value. It was awful. What did he do wrong? He didn't hire a private guard to watch the house for three days. But who does that? The police said it was a very odd situation (most thieves aren't willing to be lethally fumigated to get your TV set), and all of Dave's friends had gone through getting fumigated without even hearing about hiring a guard. Though the failure had been preventable, it was so unusual that he accepted it as merely a screwup. Huge, painful, and expensive, but—just a screwup.

Then he had to stay up half the night (again) to get his budget in on time the next day. Dave is a famous procrastinator. He has lots of tricks to solve this persistent failing, and they work a good 7 percent of the time. He's learned to work around it most of the time and just live with it the rest of the time. He almost never misses a deadline—he just gets to stay up late a lot. Big deal. There's apparently not much left to learn here. Been there, still doing that. It's a weakness.

He was very surprised while talking on the phone to a client not long ago. Dave had just opened the conversation with a marketing question about the project they were working on when the client lost her temper and started yelling. Dave was floored. He'd not heard that the key engineer on the project had quit and everything was in shambles. Though it was the scheduled reason for his call, his lengthy opening question about marketing was now irrelevant, and the client was furious that he was wasting her time. That is *not* the sort of mistake Dave is used to making. He's actually pretty great at client management, and talks on the phone a few dozen hours a week. So what happened this time? As he thought about it, he realized that the mistake was launching right into the agenda of the call without checking in first. Almost all Dave's calls are scheduled with an agenda topic and a tight time frame. He usually has great success if he launches into the agenda right away, but now he realized that he never does that when he meets people in person.

In a live meeting, he starts with a check-in to see how the person is and what news has developed since their last contact, and he always confirms the agenda before getting down to business. He often discovers important news during that check-in, but he stopped doing it some time ago on the phone, in the interest of saving time. Skipping it was clearly a risk; he just hadn't gotten caught until now. The insight was clear—do a quick news-and-agenda check, even in phone calls. It only takes a few seconds and can make a huge difference.

Dave needed less time to analyze those five failures than it took you to read about them. This exercise is not hard, but it can bring big rewards. If Dave had just left that bad phone call saying, "Sheesh! What's her problem, anyway?," he'd have learned nothing and would still be at risk of doing it again. Similarly, if he'd not thought about what led to that awful robbery or blowing his daughter's birthday, he would still be beating himself up about those situations needlessly—to no productive end.

A little failure reframing can go a long way to building up your failure immunity. Give it a try.

Don't Fight Reality

Even if you have your dream job and your dream life, stuff will still hit the fan. Designers know a lot about how things don't work out as planned. When you understand who you are, design your life, and then go live your life, you cannot fail. It does not mean that you won't stumble or that a particular prototype will always work as expected. But failure immunity comes from knowing that a prototype that did not work still leaves you with valuable information about the state of the world *here*—at your new starting point. When obstacles happen, when your progress gets derailed, when the prototype changes unexpectedly—life design lets you turn absolutely any change, setback, or surprise into something that can contribute to who you are becoming personally and professionally.

Life designers don't fight reality. They become tremendously empowered by designing their way forward no matter what. In life design, there are no wrong choices; there are no regrets. There are just prototypes, some that succeed and some that fail. Some of our greatest learning comes from a failed prototype, because then we know what to build differently next time. Life is not about winning and losing. It's about learning and playing the infinite game, and when we approach our lives as designers, we are constantly curious to discover what will happen next.

The only question that remains is one we've all heard a time or two before: What would you do if you knew you could not fail?

Try Stuff
Reframing Failure

1. **Using the worksheet below (or downloading it from www.designingyour.life), look back over the last week (or month or year), and log your failures.**
2. **Categorize them as screwups, weaknesses, or growth opportunities.**
3. **Identify your growth insights.**
4. **Build a habit of converting failures to growth by doing this once or twice a month.**

Failure	Screwup	Weakness	Growth Opportunity	Insight

11

Building a Team

Every great design was made great because there was a design team that brought that project, product, or building to life. Designers believe in radical collaboration because true genius is a collaborative process. We design our lives in collaboration and connection with others, because *we* is always stronger than *I*—it's as simple as that.

Dysfunctional Belief: *It's my life, I have to design it myself.*
Reframe: *You live and design your life in collaboration with others.*

When you design your life, you are engaging in an act of co-creation. When you use design thinking, the mind-set is completely different from "career development" or "strategic planning" or even "life coaching." One key difference is the role of community. If you're the sole architect of your brilliant future, then you think the whole thing up and you heroically bring it into being—it's all about you. Life design is about your life, but it's not all about you—it's all about us. When we say we can't do this alone, we don't just mean that we'd like to do it ourselves but we're insufficient, so we have to go get some helpers. What we mean is that life design is intrinsically a communal effort. When you are wayfinding a step or two at a time to build (not solve) your way forward, the process has to rely on the contribution and participation of others. The ideas and opportunities you design are not just presented to you or fetched for you by others on your behalf— they are *co-created with you* in collaboration with the whole community of players you engage with in life. Whether they think of it this way or not, all the people you meet, engage, prototype, or converse with along the way are in your design community. A few particularly important people will become your core collaborators and play a crucial and ongoing part in your life design, but everyone matters.

Everyone.

Co-creation is an integral aspect of a design point of view, and it's a key reason that design thinking works. Your life design isn't in you; it's in the world, where you will discover and co-create it with others. The ideas and possibilities and roles and forms that you will end up living do not actually exist anywhere in the universe right now, as you are reading this. They are all waiting to be invented, and the raw material to invent them is found out in the world and, most important, lying in wait in the hearts and minds and actions of others—many of whom you've not met yet. A big reason so many traditional approaches to doing this sort of work are unsuccessful is that they're based on the false perception that you (and you alone) know the answers, you have the resources, and you know the right passion to follow in order to have it all.

You know the kind of thinking we're talking about here—the kind that says you should set some good goals and go get it. It sounds like the locker room at halftime: "Get out there! *You can do it!*"

We say that's nuts.

Think about Ellen, Janine, and Donald from our introduction. They had goals. Janine and Donald had accomplished many of their goals, and quite successfully. But both of them were lost in their own ways—wondering why they weren't happy with their choices, wondering which direction to go next, and not knowing how to make the actual living of their lives matter in a way that made sense. And all three of them believed they had to figure it out all alone. They weren't designing their lives, and they weren't using a team.

If you find yourself standing alone in front of the mirror trying to solve or figure out your life, waiting to make a move until you are clear about the correct answers, you're going to be waiting a long time.

Look away from the mirror, and look at the people around you. If you've been doing the work and the exercises suggested throughout this book, you've already engaged lots of people— many of whom you just met. You talked to others honestly about your current situation, your values, your Workview and Lifeview. You've identified groups and individuals who are part of your energy-producing activities in your Good Time Journal. You probably had some helpers for ideating or getting feedback on your alternative life plans. People appear in every single one of your prototypes as collaborators, participants, and informers. You may not have thought of all these people as being a part of your team. You may have just thought of them as the people who were there when you were doing or trying stuff.

That would be missing the point.
They are part of your team.

Identifying Your Team

Everyone participating in your life design effort in one way or another should be thought of as being a part of your team, but there are different roles to be played, and it's useful to name them. And, yes, of course, certain individuals will appear in more than one of these roles:

Supporters. Supporters come in all flavors, ages, proximities, and sizes. Supporters are just those go-to people you can count on to care about your life—people close enough to you that their encouragement helps keep you going and their feedback is of real use. Most of your supporters are people you think of as your friends, but not all friends are supporters, and some supporters are not friends (they are there for you in your life design, but you don't hang out with them). How many supporters you have is largely a result of your personality—this group may range from two or three to fifty or even a hundred.

Players. Players are the active participants in your life design projects—especially your ongoing work-related and avocational projects and prototypes. These are the people you actually do things with, your co-workers in the classic sense.

Intimates. Intimates include your immediate and close extended family members and your closest friends. These are likely the people most directly affected by your life design, and, whether or not they are actively involved with your life design project, they are the most influential people in it. We encourage you at least to keep your intimates informed, if not directly involved, in your life design work. These people are a big part of your life, so don't leave them out. What role to have them play in your ideation, planning, and prototyping can be tricky. Some of them may be too close. Some of them may have a preference for a certain result so well established that they can't be objective. And, of course, some of them are the best helpers you could possibly ask for. All we're saying is that you recognize how important these people are and figure out an effective and appropriate role for them. Do try to avoid the mistake of leaving them completely out of it until the end. That seldom works out well, for a lot of reasons you can probably imagine. Surprising your wife with the fact that you're prototyping living off the grid for the next year is not going to land well.

The Team. These are the people with whom you're sharing the specifics of your life design project and who will track with you on that project over time at regular intervals. The most likely candidates for your team are among the people you invited to your feedback session to present and discuss your three alternative five-year Odyssey Plans.

You need a group of people to walk alongside you as you are doing your life design. They don't have to be your best friends. They just need to be willing to show up for you, to be helpfully attentive and reflective with you, and to respect and care about the process—but not full of answers and advice.

You know the kind of folks we mean; their faces are already coming to mind. A healthy team is more than two people and not more than six, including you; optimally, your team would be three to five people. Just one person can be a great partner or an accountability buddy, but two people make a pair, not a team. In a pair, there's always one speaker and one listener. A hundred percent of the response to what's just been said is on the shoulders of the other person. A pair does not create enough diversity of opinion for the kind of collaboration you need.

When there are three people in the circle, a much more active dynamic is at play, and a truly wide-ranging conversation can ensue. That process continues up to maybe even six people, and then it starts to shift again. Beyond six people, there's limited airtime for each participant. Who speaks next becomes an issue. Since everyone's time is limited and we hear less from each person, roles start to form. Ann becomes the practical one; Theo is always defending your creative side. On bigger teams, each person gets stuck in a persona, and the conversation shrinks. So, again, try to build a team of three to five people for the best dynamics and most innovative input (and just one extra-large pizza will do for team sessions—and that's always a plus).

Team Roles and Rules

First of all, keep it simple. The team's focus is on supporting an effective life design—no more and no less. The team members are not your therapist, your financial adviser, or your spiritual guru. They are your co-creators in your life design. The only role that really needs to be defined is that of the team facilitator—the person who organizes when you get together and what you do when you meet. Usually, that's you. It's best if you drive the scheduling and communications; that way, you can be sure the team is on track and not doing too much or too little. But you may ask another member to actually facilitate the meetings, or you may pass that role around. It doesn't really matter, as long as someone is always keeping an eye on the clock, the agenda, and the conversation.

That last part—the conversation—is the most important. The role is to be a facilitator, not a boss or a referee or a "leader." You don't need any of those. You just want someone to participate in the conversation and also attend to how it's going—making sure that everyone is heard from and that key ideas and suggestions aren't lost in the noise, and helping the team determine which path to follow when multiple issues or considerations present themselves at once (which happens a lot). As far as rules go, we use just four in our Stanford teams (which we call sections).

Keep it:

1. **Respectful**
2. **Confidential**
3. **Participative (no holding back)**
4. **Generative (constructive, not skeptical or judging)**

Calling All Mentors

Mentors play a very special role in your life design community or team. Not everyone reading this book has had access to a good mentoring experience, but some of you have, and we urge everyone to try to find it. Your life design effort will be greatly enhanced if you've got a few mentors participating with you. Mentoring has become popular in recent years, and here are a few things we've discovered about mentoring that have been most helpful to our students and clients.

Counsel and Advice. We make a clear distinction between counsel and advice. "Counsel" is when someone is trying to help you figure out what you think. "Advice" is when someone is telling you what he or she thinks. Fortunately, there's a very easy way to tell when you're getting advice rather than counsel.

When someone says, "Well . . . If I were you, I would blah, blah, blah"—anytime you hear "If I were you"—you're getting advice. When someone says, "If I were you," what he really means is "If you were me." See, that's the point of advice—telling you to do in your life what the adviser would do in your situation. Well, that's great if you happen to be identical to the person giving the advice. If you are a genetic twin, go for it. Otherwise, we seldom find ourselves advising people who are just like us. Advice is fine to get—you just want to be very careful about actually taking it. If you're getting advice, try to find out the adviser's values and priorities and point of view, and what key experiences informed the evolution of her conviction about that advice.

We know an ER doctor who emphatically advises everyone, "Don't *ever* ride a motorcycle—you'll just become an organ donor!" From a person who sees lots of motorcycle accident victims come into her ER, and too many of them dead of brain injuries, that's very understandable and rational advice. But we also know a fine artist on the East Coast whose inspirations for his very successful oil paintings have all come from his up-close encounters while motorcycling around the country for thirty to a hundred thousand miles a year—for thirty years. He's convinced that the best way to see the world and meet the people in it is from the back of a motorcycle (an old-school flathead Harley-Davidson, preferably). They're both right: Motorcycles are much more dangerous than cars. Motorcycling is a great way to see the countryside and meet people. Both are true. What's important is, how does that advice relate to you?

Good advice comes from people who have indisputable expertise. You want an expert to advise you on filing your taxes, or whether you should have surgery or just physical therapy for that bum knee. There is no expert adviser for your life. People will sometimes say, "I got bad advice." That's probably not true; they just got good advice that didn't fit. Lots of people will be ready to give you advice on your life. Be very careful about that.

Counsel is entirely different. Counsel is always helpful. You can never be too clear on your own thinking. You can never get too good a grasp of your own best wisdom and insights. Finding someone who can give you good counsel and who regularly leaves you in a clearer and more settled state of mind is a great asset. This is where good mentors shine. We would say that all legitimate mentoring is centered on giving counsel. Counsel invariably begins with lots of questions aimed at accurately understanding you, what you're saying, and what you're going through. Good counselors will often seem to ask the same question a couple of times from different points of view, to be sure they're getting it. They will often try to summarize or restate something you've said and ask, "Did I get that right?" This approach tells you that they're focused on you—not on themselves.

The value of mentors' life experience when they are giving counsel lies not in borrowing what facts or answers they know but in accessing the breadth of their experience and their objectivity, which helps them to help you to see your own reality in a new way. Good mentors spend most of their time listening, then offering possible reframings of your situation that allow you to have new ideas and come up with the answers that will work for you.

Of course, this is just our advice.

Discernment. We talked about discernment in chapter 9, when we discussed making good decisions by employing multiple ways of knowing. Mentors can make a particularly valuable contribution to your discernment process when it's time to make choices. Important decisions are seldom easy, and there are lots of competing issues and trade-off considerations that conspire to make it awfully noisy in your head. When you've got a noisy brain, that's a great time to connect with a mentor who can counsel you. The mentor can listen to you dump out all the stuff going on inside you and help you to make sense of it all, sorting it into the big stuff, the small stuff, and the irrelevant stuff. A good mentor will do this with some care, and even some trepidation. Sorting and prioritizing issues often comes very close to pointing someone toward a preferred choice. A good mentor will resist telling you what to do, or will at least be explicitly cautious about the risks of overinfluencing you. She might say, "Well, look, I'm really not trying to tell you that I think the right thing is to take that promotion and move to Beijing for a year, but I do notice that every time you talk about China you light up and you smile. Have you noticed that? If so, you probably should just take a look at that. I'm not saying go to China; I just think there's something there worth noticing."

The Long View and the Local View. Mentors come in lots of forms. Some people are fortunate enough to find a lifelong mentor, someone who really cares about their lives and is committed to walking with them throughout their journey for years and years. But that's not the only kind of valuable mentor. You can find topical mentors (parenting, finances, spirituality, etc.), and you can find ad hoc or seasonal mentors (getting through the pregnancy, handling your first managerial role, dealing with elderly parents, moving to Costa Rica). There really are no rules here—just be on the lookout for people who can provide mentoring assistance to you.

Now, you're probably wondering where you are going to find all these great mentors. (If you're not, then skip this part; you are one of the lucky ones who are well stocked with mentors.) We suggest that there are many more people capable of giving good mentoring than there are good mentors. Lots of people with significant life experience and the willingness to listen and provide counsel (not just advice) are out there, but many of them don't think of themselves as mentors, or aren't skilled in the practice of a mentoring conversation. It's not that these people aren't mentors—they are just not what we call master mentors.

This is where being a good *mentee* comes in. You don't need 100 percent master mentors. Sure, master mentors are great, and if you've got some, hang on to them. But all you really need are mentor-capable people from whom you can extract a mentor contribution. It's surprisingly easy to do. You just have to be the initiator. When you identify someone who you think can serve you as a mentor, find a way to spend some time with the person and direct the conversation to the areas in which you want help. Specifically, ask him not so much to tell you what he'd do as to use his insights and experience to try to help you sort out your own thinking.

"Hey, Harold. I really appreciate the way you and Louise have raised your kids, and, frankly, this whole father thing scares the heck outta me. Could I buy you a cup of coffee just to hear some of your stories about that sometime?"

Of course, Harold will say yes (and, yes, this approach is strikingly similar to how we set up a prototype conversation in chapter 6). When you get together, after you have Harold tell you some of the endearing and some of the scary fathering moments he recalls, you just ask, "I wonder if you could do this for me. I've got a situation brewing with Skippy, and Lucy and I are kind of flummoxed about it. What if I just tell you what we've got on our minds, and maybe you could help me hear my own best thoughts on this? I think Skippy is pretty different from any of your and Louise's kids, but you've got a practiced father's ear, and maybe you could help me sort out the majors from the minors of what we're dealing with here."

That may be a different role from anything Harold is used to, but he'll give it his best shot and probably do pretty well. If he veers into advice, just listen respectfully and come back to the request. He'll probably get it; if he doesn't, nothing lost and you can try someone else. This way, you can build your own stable of mentors without having to wait for one of the master mentors to appear on the horizon.

Beyond Team to Community

If you're like most of the people we've worked with, you'll find the time you spend with your Life Design Team and collaborators to be pretty stimulating and life-giving. The kind of support and sincere and respectful listening that we're hoping you're experiencing as you do this are pretty habit-forming. There is something incredibly special about being part of a community. It's how humans are supposed to live.

Community is more than just sharing resources or hanging out now and then. It's showing up and investing in the ongoing creation of one another's lives. Being in that kind of community is a great way to live, and we highly recommend it as an ongoing practice, not just when making big plans or starting new things.

Identifying what sustaining practices will help keep you growing and enjoying your well-designed life is an important part of the formula, and community is an important piece.

So what exactly do we mean by a "community" when we're talking about an ongoing experience, not just your ad hoc Life Design Team? Once upon a time, a majority of people found themselves organically located in a community. They were raised in a church or a faith tradition. They were part of a large extended family that actively gathered regularly and in particular ways. They may have been participants in a career, such as the military, or an avocation, such as rock climbing, that brought a community with it. But today most people do not have a ready-made community—a place to return to regularly where they can have this kind of life conversation. To find a "community" as we intend it, you're looking for a group of people that shares most of the following attributes:

Kindred Purpose. Healthy communities are about something—not just getting together to get together. Dave's community exists to become people of greater integrity in living out their faith in all aspects of their lives. Bill's community gathers to support one another in becoming better fathers and more authentic men. The most effective communities have an explicit mission that keeps them directed and moving. It's just much easier to keep moving if you're moving toward something. Both Bill's and Dave's communities veer into all manner of other stuff—social activities, recreational events, and the like—but there is always that North Star pulling them back to "why we're here."

Meets Regularly. Whether at the same time every week or month or quarter or not, the community must meet regularly. It must gather frequently enough to sustain a consistent, ongoing conversation in which the members can pick up where they left off last time without starting all over again and again. The real intention here is that participation in the community becomes a practice in and of itself. The community isn't just gathering for the ad hoc purpose of getting a project done or finishing reading the book together—it gathers because its participants agree that a life lived in a community-supported way is a better designed life, and they stick with it. Neither of us could have ended up in the lives we now live had it not been for the ongoing practice of this kind of community.

Shared Ground. If possible, in addition to a kindred purpose, it's helpful to have other shared ground. This is usually in the form of values or point of view. In Bill's dads' discussion group, most of the guys share the hope of being better dads than they had themselves; they are committed to total honesty (there's a *No BS* rule); and they all are willing to try new things and "do the work," including trying crazy exercises—such as asking someone to play dead, then talking about him as if they were at his funeral. As long as you're alive it's not too late to revise the potential content of your eulogy, so each member listens and can then decide if he likes who he's become or not. This explicit shared ground keeps the group together, keeps the conversation going, and acts as a means of establishing priorities and mediating issues as the group journeys together. Even though no more than a shared affection ("getting along well") and a willingness to participate may be enough to get started, we've seldom seen that be enough to hold people together for the long haul.

To Know and Be Known. Some groups are all about the content or the process, and some groups are all about the people. We are talking about a community that's at least in large part about the people. You can be in a really great book club, where people do the reading and show up prepared and have thoughtful discussions on writing, narrative, and the state of civil society plus a little wine tasting on the side, and you all really like one another, and it's *great.* But that's not a community as we mean it. It really is great—don't get us wrong. It has a purpose (informed book discussions), it has shared ground (reading novels makes us more interesting, thoughtful, and open-minded), and it meets regularly (first Tuesday of the month)—but we aren't engaged in one another's lives, and we don't actually have to know one another at all to make the community work. That great book club would not likely be a place *to have this conversation.* A community doesn't have to be made up entirely of intimates, but there should be some level of personal disclosure about what each person is up to and how it's going.

What makes an effective community is not having people in it with the right expertise or information. What makes it work is people with the right intention and presence. It is most helpful to be with people who are trying to connect the dots and live in coherence with themselves and the world in an honest way. Being around a dentist who is doing a sincere job of turning into her best self is more encouraging and impactful, despite your being totally uninterested in dentistry, than being in community with someone who has exactly the same interests and career aspirations as you but who isn't being sincerely present and engaging honestly with his hopes and struggles. You don't need everyone to strip emotionally naked, but you want a group in which you're going to be known and you're going to know others at a level where you feel like you're all in this together.

Here's a way to test what we mean. Think of the different groups you've participated in over the years. You can probably think of groups in which the people were talking about ideas about their lives, and groups in which the people were actually talking about their lives. It's the difference between commentators and participants. It's a community of participants that you're looking for.

Our hope for this book is that it will help you find or create such a community. By all means, read it at your next book club, but then find those who are willing to go on this journey with you. Life design *is* a journey, and it's really not as much fun to travel alone.

For now, we want you to know that we consider you part of our team, and invite you to be a part of our community. Find out how to do that here (www.designingyour.life).

Try Stuff
Building a Team

1. Make a list of three to five people who might be a part of your Life Design Team. Think of your supporters, your intimates, your mentors or possible mentors. Ideally, these will be three to five people also actively engaged in designing their lives.

2. Make sure everyone has a copy of the book (or buy books for everyone), so all the members of your team understand how life design works and have reviewed the team roles and rules.

3. Agree to meet regularly and actively to co-create a well-designed life as a community.

Conclusion

A Well-Designed Life

What does a well-designed and balanced life look like? Imagine a day cut into perfectly equal pieces of pie—one slice for career, one slice for play and fun, one slice for family and friends, one slice for health. What is your perfect pie? We all know the areas of our lives that are in need of a little more time and effort, and could benefit from a little more design thinking and a little less worry, rumination, and should've/would've/could've thinking.

Now, how much of your day today did you actually spend having some fun? Advancing your career? Nurturing your relationships? Taking care of your health? Prototyping what's next? What does your pie *really* look like?

Let us tell you a little secret. There is no perfect pie. It is virtually impossible on any given day to devote yourself equally to all the areas of your life that are important to you.

Balance happens over time.

Life design happens over time.

Bill Gates, the world's richest man (as of 2015), did not get that way by having work/love balance on any given day. When he launched Microsoft Windows in 1985 and took the company public in 1986, no one would have called him a philanthropist doing good in the world. And it's also probably safe to say that back in 1998 he wasn't spending an equal part of his day nurturing relationships and an equal part defending government charges against him for abusing monopoly power.

Balance is a myth, and it causes a lot of grief and heartache for most of us.

As we said earlier, we don't fight reality, and living in reality means looking at and accepting where you are right now. Life design is really about being able to answer the question "How's it going?"

It is possible to design your life in such a way that when those closest to you are giving your eulogy they will say, "Overall, he had a pretty evenly sliced pie."

Okay, so maybe you don't want someone to say exactly *that* in your eulogy, but you get the idea. We know we don't want someone to stand up at our funerals and say, "Dave had good written and verbal communication skills." Or "Bill really demonstrated the ability to juggle competing priorities and move quickly." Life is about more than a paycheck and job performance. We all want to know we mattered to someone. We all want to know our work contributed to the world. We all want to know we loved and we lived the best we could, with as much purpose and meaning as possible, and that we had a pretty fun time doing it.

And you only understand that in retrospect, because a well-designed life isn't a noun—it's a verb (technically it is a noun phrase but you know what we mean).

Dysfunctional Belief: *I finished designing my life; the hard work is done, and everything will be great.*
Reframe: *You never finish designing your life—life is a joyous and never-ending design project of building your way forward.*

Some of you are reading this book to improve a life that's already pretty okay; others are reading this book as part of a significant transition that you've either intended or that reality has thrust upon you. You have important plans to execute, you have choices to make, and once you do that, your life will be quite different from what it used to be. In that sense, your new design will be in place and the old design will be behind you—and that shift is indeed a big deal. You can really feel it. But your life designing is not over.

So, if wayfinding is how you found your way into the life design you want to live, then it's also the way to live it. Just keep building your way forward. Design isn't just a technique to address problems and projects—it's a way of living. One of the reasons that design thinking has worked so well in our Designing Your Life classes and consulting is that it's so human. In 1963, when Stanford first began teaching design, it was with the unique approach of conceiving "human-centered design" (HCD). At the time, this was a significant departure from classical design methodologies, which were skill-centered, or art-centered, or engineering-centered, or manufacturing-centered. And the early work that went into developing the Stanford design methodology did a very good job of keeping humanness at the center of things and getting the humanity part right. Since your life is a decidedly human enterprise, it makes sense that human-centered design applies well.

Further, in life design we only take on the question of *how* to design your life—not what life you should live or why one life is better than another.

Our friend Tim graduated from college with a degree in electrical engineering and went to work in Silicon Valley. His first job was in a fast-pace, just-gone-public start-up where he was designing cutting-edge microprocessors. However, after his first design project got canceled, Tim re-evaluated all those long nights and weekends and came to the conclusion that work was not going to be the main focus of his life. He valued play and love much more, and realized that he needed to make some changes.

He switched jobs to a more mature company, rose to a comfortable senior position, and then just stayed there. He's been in that role for almost twenty years, having become very well respected as a technical guru in his firm, and has turned down promotions and the money that comes with one again and again.

"You have to make enough money to pay the bills and have the things you need," says Tim. In his case, this means supporting his family, making sure his kids have access to a great education, and having a nice house in Berkeley. "After that, what's the point? I'd rather have more fun and more friends. Money, promotions, and more responsibility do not motivate me. The point of having a good life is to be happy, not to work."

Tim's design is working, and he's one of the most balanced guys we know. He is a great dad and the center of a vibrant social life, has lots of friends, plays music almost every week, has his own cocktail blog, on which he promotes his cocktail inventions, reads a lot, and is one of the happiest people you'll ever meet. His health/

work/play/love dashboard is full of green lights, and he plans to keep it that way. And he's a great example of a well-thought-out life design strategy in which work isn't the most important thing.

Disrupting Life

Some of the reframes we've offered may be disruptive; unlearning things is often harder and more important than learning things. But we'll wager that none of what you've learned or unlearned in your sojourn through this book with us—as disruptive or obvious or upsetting or enlightening as it might be—will actually turn you into a different person. We anticipate that it will just make you more like you. This is what good design always does: it releases the best of what was already there waiting to be found and revealed. Since the foundation of our design methodology is and always has been an explicitly human process that is applied iteratively, it stands to reason that it offers not only an innovative approach to conceiving the life you want but a way to go about living it as well. Which brings us back to the five mind-sets.

We introduced the idea of life design in this book by telling you five simple things you need to do: (1) be curious (curiosity), (2) try stuff (bias to action), (3) reframe problems (reframing), (4) know it's a process (awareness), and (5) ask for help (radical collaboration). We've reminded you of these mind-sets throughout the book as we've walked through the various ideas and tools that constitute life design.

You can apply some of the five mind-sets virtually anywhere, on any given day. The opportunities to live into being curious or to try stuff are endless. We run an exercise in our classes called Designing Your Way Forward, in which we have our students identify two or three things in their life design project that they are stuck on, things that are going nowhere fast. We then ask them to ideate for four minutes on that stuck problem with two other students, who will help them apply any one of the five mind-sets as a way to get unstuck. How can "be curious" help you overcome the fear of talking to the Nobel Prize–winning professor who teaches your class? Well . . . you could: Ask three other students who met with her what they talked about and how it went. See if she talks about her own college experience anywhere in some article or interview, and if her twenty-year-old self shares anything with yours. Find out if she's ever failed miserably at some projects (and what they were if so), to make her seem more human and less scary. And so on. When we do this, it turns out that applying any of the mind-sets can help you get unstuck and take some progressive next steps. The same is true for the well-lived life you're now trying to engage. Here are some reminders for each of the mind-sets.

Be Curious. There's something interesting about everything. Endless curiosity is key to a well-designed life. Nothing is boring to everyone (even doing taxes or washing the dishes).

What would someone who's interested in this want to know?
How does it work?
Why do they do it that way?
How did they used to do it?
What do experts in this field argue about and why?
What's the most interesting thing going on here?

What don't I get about what's happening here?
How could I find out?

Try Stuff. With a bias to action, there is no more being stuck—no more worrying, analyzing, pondering, or solving your way through life. Just do it.

How can we try this before the day is out?
What would we like to know more about?
What can I do that will answer that?
What sorts of things are actionable, and if we tried them, what might we learn?

Reframe Problems. Reframing is a change in perspective, and almost any design problem can use a perspective switch.

What perspective do I actually have?
Where am I now coming from?
What other perspectives could other people have? Name them, and then describe the problem from their perspective, not yours.

Redescribe your problem using some of the following reframe lenses: Your problem is actually very small. Very easy to fix. An opportunity more than a problem. Something you can just skip entirely. Something you actually don't understand at all yet. Not your problem. And how will it look a year later?

Know It's a Process. Awareness of the process means you don't get frustrated or lost, and you don't ever give up.

What are all the steps behind you and in front of you that you
   can imagine?
Is what's on your mind actually germane to the step you're on
   now?
Are you on the right step, or are you ahead of or behind yourself?
What happens if you don't think more than one step ahead?
What's the worst thing that can happen? How likely is it to hap-
   pen, and what would you do if it did?
What's the best thing that can happen?

   Write down all the questions, worries, ideas, and hopes that
you have, and then ask yourself if you know what to do next.
Does it feel different now?

   Ask for Help. Radical collaboration means that you aren't
alone in the process. Find a supporter you can talk to about what
you're in the midst of—right now. Tell this person your situation
for five minutes, and ask for five minutes of feedback and discussion. How do you feel now (regardless of what your supporter
said—just talking to someone other than yourself)? There are lots
of ways to get collaboration started:

Build a team.
Create a community.
Who are all the different groups and constituencies involved in
   what you're working on? Are you connected to and in conversation with all of them? If not—get going.
Keep an ask-for-help journal in which you jot down the questions you want help on, and keep it handy. Each week, identify
   some people who can help you with some of the journal entries

and reach out to them. Journal answers and results from your helpers.

Find a mentor.

Call your mother (she'd love it—you know she would).

If you try to keep the mind-sets as an active orientation to how you're living and use them as part of your life design implementation as well as part of your innovation process, you'll very quickly get the hang of it. It's a simple list, and it takes almost no effort to bring these mind-sets to the forefront of your thinking and see if they can serve you. In short order, you'll find a natural, organic adoption of the mind-sets as part of your own way.

Just Two More Things

Beyond the five mind-sets, there are two more things that you particularly want to pay attention to in living your well-designed life—your compass and your practices. Your compass is about those great big organizing ideas of your Workview and Lifeview. These, along with your values, provide the foundation for your answer to "How's it going?" They inform you if you are on a good track for you, or are out of sync with yourself. They determine if you're living a coherent life in which you've got *who you are, what you believe,* and *what you're doing* in adequate alignment. When we talk to our students two, three, five, or more years after they've graduated and left our class, they say that their compass is one of the exercises they keep coming back to. Most of us find that our primary views on these questions stay fairly constant, but the specifics and the nuances and the priorities do change, and it's very helpful to stay on top of that. The best way to know what you really think and value about the big questions of life is to ask yourself and see what you have to say. We urge you to revisit your compass at least annually, and recalibrate it. This will help you revitalize the creation of meaning in your life.

Perhaps the most important recommendation we can give you to sustain a well-designed life is to invest in and commit to some *personal practices* of the variety we described in chapter 9. In our own lives, both of us would say that our personal growth in this area—the refinement and disciplined participation in practices— has been the single most life-giving thing we've done. Even though appreciation of the value of such practices (yoga, medita- tion, poetry writing/reading, prayer, etc.) is gaining ground, this remains an area of great weakness, especially in modern society. Traditional Eastern cultures are better at it, but, frankly, almost no modern cultures excel here. The good news is that even a small effort can bring great results. By educating your emotions and maturing your discernment through such practices, you stand to reap great benefits that are accessible on an almost daily basis.

For example, Bill is nourished by a morning meditation (done while shaving) and the daily affirmation he referred to on his health dashboard: "I live in the best of all possible worlds. Every- thing I do today, I choose to do." And then he recounts in his mind everything in front of him that day, reminds himself that all those things are things he put there, and then re-chooses them before entering the day. He also now dedicates significant time each week to painting and drawing to animate his creative brain and experience the pure joy of it. And he makes at least one complex if not gourmet meal a week, to do something creative that others can share in.

Dave works to spend twenty minutes a day in silent meditation (technically "centering prayer") to recenter himself in the love of God. He also now reads poetry at least once a week, trying to learn how to feel the poem in his body, not just read it in his head. He relies on his erudite wife, Claudia, to curate his poetry assignments, since he cleverly designed a marriage with a much smarter spouse. And he forgoes the speed and thrill of road cycling as exercise once a week to walk in the hills for at least four miles with Claudia and the dogs, to slow things down and see nature more intimately.

These are some of the things we do, but we hope you will build and prototype your own set of practices to find what works for you and helps you to live your own well-designed life.

So—How's It Going?

At the beginning of this book, we introduced you to Ellen who liked rocks, Janine the misplaced lawyer, and Donald the lost manager. How did life design change the way they used to answer the difficult question "How's it going?" into the way they answer it now?

Ellen knew she didn't want to be a geologist, but she also knew that she loved some parts of what she learned in school, especially the organizing and cataloguing that come with being a geologist. And she still liked rocks, especially the fine gems used in jewelry. So she decided to get good at being lucky and started Life Design Interviewing. She discovered that project management jobs require people who excel at organizing and categorizing tasks and people. That felt like a fit to her. After a few more interviews, she networked her way to a start-up that was doing, among other things, online jewelry auctions. Her love of "rocks" and her natural organizational talent came through in the conversation, and her curiosity about the company really stood out. The Life Design Interview quickly turned into a job interview. Two years and several promotions later, she is now the account manager for everything the company does in their high-fashion auction business.

Janine really worked on her compass and developed personal practices that helped her to recognize and trust her own inner voice. She found journaling life-giving and eventually recognized that the reason journaling had become so important to her was that she is a writer—a poet, actually. After she had been working on her writing on the side for a time, she and her husband decided it was time for her to "go for it," and she entered an M.F.A. poetry graduate program; she has now begun a new (and frugal) life as a speaker, writer, and poet.

Donald used the mind-set of curiosity to reframe his complaint, "Why the hell am I doing this?," into a new question, "What is so interesting around there that it keeps all these people coming back to this company day after day?" He followed that question into lots of Life Design Interviews with his colleagues, looking for the ones who were really enjoying themselves and had figured out just what the hell they *were* doing there. When he combined his insights from those stories with the results from his Good Time Journal, the pattern was clear. The way to get re-energized was to refocus on the people. He discovered that he wasn't in the wrong place, he was just in the wrong state of mind. He'd gotten so preoccupied with the *what* and the *how* of business success and family responsibilities that he'd completely forgotten the *why* and the *who*. He reinvented himself without having to change anything about his situation. Reframing his work from "getting the job done" to "creating a dynamic culture where my employees love their work" was transformative.

Neither Ellen, Janine, nor Donald (nor Clara, Elise, Kurt, Chung, or . . .) used all the tools, but they all took up the challenge, got unstuck, and built their way forward. We are grateful to have known them and to have been a small part of their lives.

We know that writing a book called *Designing Your Life* gives each of us the opportunity to be either a living example of how this stuff works or a big hypocrite. We each put these ideas and tools to work on a daily basis, and we are constantly prototyping new exercises, new ways of thinking, and new ways of living into a well-designed life. We have shared with you some of our daily practices, and encourage you to go to our website (www.designingyour.life) for a complete list of daily practices you might like to try.

Our lives are constantly evolving—from engineers, to consultants, to teachers, to authors—and with each step of the journey we are constantly grateful and perpetually curious to see what our well-designed life will look like next.

Throughout this book, we've shared with you the stories of many people we've worked with and gotten to know along the way. Though not everyone is "living the dream," we can say with an informed confidence that every one of our collaborators who has put into practice at least some (if not all) of these tools and ideas has made real progress in ways none of them had experienced before.

We have enjoyed a long and radical collaboration with each other and with thousands of students and clients who have embarked on the journey of life design with us, and we look forward to collaborating with you.

We hope you will let us know how it's going, but, more important, we hope you are able to answer "How's it going?" satisfyingly for yourself.

Life design is ultimately a way of life that will transform how you look at your life and how you live your life. The end result of a well-designed life is a life well lived.

And, really, is there anything more we could hope for?

Acknowledgments

There are many people who have been important and encouraging on the road to writing this book. At the great risk of leaving someone out, we wish to acknowledge:

Eugene Korsunskiy and Kyle Williams, our founding Life Design Fellows, for believing in us and for working hard in their crucial role getting the Lab started.

The Stanford d.Life Fellows Jon Kleiman, Gabriel Lomeli, Gabriel Wilson, Kristin Mayer, Kathy Davies, Gabrielle Santa-Donato, and Lauren Pizer for embodying "radical collaboration" and helping grow Designing Your Life into a gift for everyone.

David Kelley, for creating the position of executive director of Stanford's Product Design program for me (Bill), letting me teach whatever I wanted, and starting the journey that led to this book.

Professor Sheri Sheppard for being a stalwart DYL supporter, heroic grad student advocate, and artful faculty mentor willing to take a gamble on a couple of guys with mere master's degrees.

To the forward-thinking leaders at Stanford who believed in the power of Life Design and paved the way for changing the university and, hopefully, higher education: Harry Elam, Ph.D., vice provost of undergraduate education; Patti Gumport, Ph.D., vice provost of graduate education; Brad Osgood, Ph.D., former dean of students, School of Engineering; Greg Boardman, vice provost of student affairs.

A special recognition to our first collaborators who partnered with us in the very early days and whose years of support and encouragement have made all the difference: Scotty McClennan, dean of religious life (retired), who modeled patience and persistence in bringing cultural change; Shari Palmer, associate vice provost of undergraduate education, who coached us on how the university thinks; Lance Choy, former executive director of the career development center, who broke it all open when he asked the seminal question "Can't you do this for *students in every major?*"; and Julie Lythcott-Haims, former dean of freshmen, who pushed us to reach out to the entire student body, energized us with reliable encouragements, and showed us the way to growing DYL beyond ourselves by becoming our first certified co-instructor.

Lindsay Oishi, Ph.D., and Tim Reilly, Ph.D., who made the huge personal investment of dedicating their doctoral research projects to demonstrating the efficacy of DYL, and in so doing set our work apart and ensured we gave people what they deserved. To Professors Dan Schwartz and Bill Damon, their advisers, for their support and guidance, and Dr. Denise Pope, founder of Challenge Success, for her careful research insights and demonstration that you can change the education system.

Randy Bare, then director of Westminster House at the University of California at Berkeley, for innocently suggesting to me (Dave) in 1999, "You should teach a course here!," and kicked off my fourth career as an educator.

Dr. Sharon Daloz-Parks, who asked me (Dave) with uncanny prescience so many years ago, "Are you ready for where this will take you?," and has never flagged in her soulful support and loving exhortation.

Bob McKim, who created the Product Design program at Stanford and rescued a lost physics major (Bill), starting me on a career that has been so much fun. And Bernie Roth, a mentor and guide, and the one person we turn to when we have to figure out university politics.

Jim Adams, who inspired both of us as undergraduate students and taught us to bust conceptual blocks, including the one he put in front of us in 2007 when he said, "I don't know how you guys could actually teach this stuff!," which spurred us to figure out how to do it.

And to those special people whose lives appear between these pages to help us show you how life design really works. We've borrowed their stories to help you write yours (and, of course, we've changed their names). For their invaluable contribution to personalizing and humanizing this book, we are forever grateful.

There are two special people who made this book possible in the most tangible way:

Lara Love, our collaborative writer, for finding the true voice of Bill-and-Dave and crafting the words we'd have written if we were real writers like she. We so appreciate her patience in enduring countless hours of meetings, videos, and recordings with no weakening of her ardor for the work or sincere affection for us. When our own energies were flagging, we could simply borrow from her bottomless well of cheerful readiness and productive availability. Lara demonstrated an incredible ability to listen deeply and then write us perfectly. She did not write for us or about us or on behalf of us. She wrote *us,* and we and every one of our readers are well served by her fine work.

Doug Abrams, our agent, book co-inventor, idea architect, publishing industry tour guide, honest friend, and all-around great collaborator. It's safe to say that without Doug this book wouldn't have happened. After our first failed attempt at writing a draft that was essentially a boring script of our class, we knew we needed help. Doug became our book design consultant and led the effort to figure out what book it really was that we had to offer the world and how to architect it well for our reader. Doug the book designer taught us what a book was. Then Doug the agent swung into action, dropped the velvet rope into the publishing world, and said, "Follow me, guys—get ready for the ride of your life." It's been a great ride so far, and we can't wait to see what comes next.

Finally, we'd like to thank the whole extraordinary team at Knopf, but one book champion at the publisher's stands alone—Vicky Wilson, our editor and chief culture change officer. We cannot describe adequately the difference it has made to have Vicky lead the charge to put this book into the world. Her commitment to the book and to us was immediate. She is a force of nature, and the book's success is unconditionally rooted in her decision to bring it into being. Her confidence in and vision for the cultural contribution *Designing Your Life* can make has been our dependable fount of renewable energy. Even experienced designers need inspiration, and Vicky has provided it to us without pause from the moment we met. Vicky, you had us at "Hello darlings . . ."—and it was one of the best things that ever happened to us. Thank you, thank you, Vicky.

Notes

Introduction: Life by Design

1. Jon Krakower, inventor of the Apple notebook configuration, see European Patent EP 0515664 B1, Laptop Computer Having Integrated Keyboard, Cursor Control Device and Palm Rest, and Artemis March, *Apple PowerBook (A): Design Quality and Time to Market,* Design Management Institute Case Study 9-994-023 (Boston: Design Management Institute Press, 1994).
2. Lindsay Oishi, "Enhancing Career Development Agency in Emerging Adulthood: An Intervention Using Design Thinking," doctoral dissertation, Graduate School of Education, Stanford University, 2012. T. S. Reilly, "Designing Life: Studies of Emerging Adult Development," doctoral dissertation, Graduate School of Education, Stanford University, 2013.
3. To learn more about these companies, visit http://embraceglobal .org and https://d-rev.org.
4. William Damon, *The Path to Purpose: How Young People Find Their Calling in Life* (New York: Free Press, 2009).

Chapter 2   Building a Compass

1. We have drawn many of our ideas and exercises from the work of the positive psychology movement, and especially from the work of Martin Seligman. The notion that "people who can make an explicit connection between their work and something socially meaningful to them are more likely to find satisfaction, and are better able to adapt to the inevitable stresses and compromises that come with working in the world" is one of the important

ideas in Seligman's book *Flourish: A Visionary New Understanding of Happiness and Well-Being* (New York: Atria Books, 2012).

Chapter 3   Wayfinding

1. For more information on the concept of flow, see *Flow: The Psychology of Optimal Experience* by Mihaly Csikszentmihalyi (New York: Harper Perennial, 2008).
2. See Suzana Herculano-Houzel's TED Talk "What's so special about the human brain?," https://www.ted.com/talks/suzana_herculano_houzel_what_is_so_special_about_the_human_brain; and Nikhil Swaminathan, "Why Does the Brain Need So Much Power?," *Scientific American,* April 29, 2008, http://www.scientificamerican.com/article/why-does-the-brain-need-s/.
3. The AEIOU framework comes from Dev Patnaik, *Needfinding: Design Research and Planning* (Amazon's CreateSpace Independent Publishing Platform, 2013).

Chapter 5   Design Your Lives

1. Steven P. Dow, Alana Glassco, Jonathan Kass, Melissa Schwarz, Daniel L. Schwartz, and Scott R. Klemmer, "Parallel Prototyping Leads to Better Design Results, More Divergence, and Increased Self-Efficacy," *ACM Transactions on Computer-Human Interactions* 17, no. 4 (Dec. 2010).
2. In addition to Homer and the Greeks, we borrowed the term "odyssey years" from David Brooks, the noted *New York Times* columnist. In his October 9, 2007, column, Brooks was describing the new realities of twenty-two-to-thirty-five-year-old Americans when he said, "With a little imagination it's possible even for baby boomers to understand what it's like to be in the middle of the *odyssey years* [italics added]. It's possible to see that this period of improvisation is a sensible response to modern

conditions." David Brooks, "The Odyssey Years," The Opinion
Pages, *New York Times,* October 9, 2007, http://www.nytimes
.com/2007/10/09/opinion/09brooks.html?_r=0.

Chapter 7   How Not to Get a Job

1. From a 2015 report, *The Recruitment Power Shift: How Candidates
   Are Powering the Economy,* on CareerBuilder, which can be found
   at http://careerbuildercommunications.com/candidatebehavior/.

Chapter 8   Designing Your Dream Job

1. https://test.naceweb.org/press/faq.aspx.

Chapter 9   Choosing Happiness

1. Peter Salovey and John D. Mayer, "Emotional Intelligence,"
   Imagination, Cognition and Personality 9 (1990): 185–211.
2. Dan Goleman is the author of *Emotional Intelligence* (New York:
   Bantam, 1995) and the follow-up book *Social Intelligence: The New
   Science of Human Relationships* (New York: Bantam, 2006) from
   which we draw the notion of the "wisdom of the emotions." For
   an informative and interesting summary of these ideas go to Dan's
   Social Intelligence Talks at Google at https://www.youtube.com
   /watch?v=-hoo_dIOP8k.
3. For more on Dan Gilbert's ideas on "synthesizing happiness"
   watch his TED Talk, "The Surprising Science of Happiness,"
   http://www.ted.com/talks/dan_gilbert_asks_why_are_we_happy
   and read *Stumbling on Happiness* (New York: Knopf, 2006).
4. For more on Barry Schwartz's ideas on choice and choosing
   watch his TED Talk, "The Paradox of Choice?," https://
   www.ted.com/talks/barry_schwartz_on_the_paradox_of
   _choice?language=en.

Chapter 10   Failure Immunity

1. Angela Duckworth's studies on grit and self-control are summarized in a great article: Daniel J. Tomasulo, "Grit: What Is It and Do You Have It?," *Psychology Today,* January 8, 2014, https://www.psychologytoday.com/blog/the-healing -crowd/201401/grit-what-is-it-and-do-you-have-it.
2. James P. Carse, *Finite and Infinite Games* (New York: Free Press, 1986).

A Note on the Type

This book was set in Adobe Garamond. Designed for the Adobe Corporation by Robert Slimbach, the fonts are based on types first cut by Claude Garamond (ca. 1480–1561). Garamond was a pupil of Geoffroy Tory and is believed to have followed the Venetian models, although he introduced a number of important differences, and it is to him that we owe the letter we now know as "old style." He gave to his letters a certain elegance and feeling of movement that won their creator an immediate reputation and the patronage of Francis I of France.

Composed by North Market Street Graphics, Lancaster, Pennsylvania
Printed and bound by Berryville Graphics, Berryville, Virginia
Designed by Iris Weinstein